of Windsurfing

THE BOOK OF
WINDSURFING
A Guide to Boardsailing Techniques

Mike Gadd
John Boothroyd
Ann Durrell

KEY PORTER BOOKS

Key Porter Books Limited
70 The Esplanade
Toronto, Ontario
Canada M5E 1R2

Design: Don Fernley
Typesetting: Compeer Typographic Services Limited
Printed and bound in Italy by Garzanti Ed., Milan
85 86 87   6 5 4 3 2 1

Canadian Cataloguing in Publication Data
Gadd, Mike.
  The book of windsurfing
Includes index.
ISBN 0-919493-53-X.

1. Windsurfing. I. Durrell, Ann, 1953–
II. Boothroyd, John, 1948–   III. Title.
GV811.63.W56G3 1985   797.1'72   C85-098002-X

To Arlene Francis Boothroyd

Contents

Preface

In the years that we have been boardsailing, the sport has mushroomed. More boards are on the market, more uses of the board have been found, and more people, young and old, are discovering this unique sport and the lifestyle that it offers.

We felt that there was a need for a clear, concise book on boardsailing (or windsurfing as it is also called). *The Book of Windsurfing* will teach beginners the basics and introduce them to competitive boardsailing, wave sailing and other exciting aspects of the sport. We hope this book will persuade you to join the world of boardsailing — a world we have come to love.

There are a number of people who have helped us with the book. We would like to thank Krista Johnson for her illustrations, Fitzwright-Sine Limited (Bare), BIC Sports, Sailfree Marketing Ltd. and Mistral. A special thank you to photographers Steve Hill, Sara Lee and Jeremy Jones.

Mike Gadd boardsailing in
the Gulf of Mexico.

A one-design race.

Introduction

The Windsurfer®, the first commercially successful sailboard.

Although a number of people claim to have invented the sailboard, the first commercially successful freesail craft (one steered by adjusting the position of the sail) was designed by James Drake, an American aeronautical engineer, and Hoyle Schweitzer, a surfing enthusiast from California. After several prototypes were built, the new invention, called the Windsurfer®, was patented and marketed beginning in 1969.

In the United States boardsailing spread from California to Hawaii, and from Florida up the New England coast. In Canada the sport began in the Kawartha Lakes region of Ontario and spread to Quebec and British Columbia. After a Dutch textile company, Ten Cate, began marketing the Windsurfer® in 1973, boardsailing became even more popular in Europe than it was in North America.

The success of the sport can be attributed to the low cost, small size and durability of the sailboard. In addition, boardsailing arrived at a time when men and women were pursuing physical fitness and moving away from motor-powered sports. Admittedly, at first the general public was skeptical. Many people didn't take the new sport seriously, dismissing it as a fad.

Today there are few large beaches in Europe or North America, or indeed throughout the world, where you will not find a boardsailing school or club promoting its activities with weeknight or weekend races. The versatility of the sailboard has led to many competitive events. Olympic triangle racing was the first one and is still popular. In 1975 the freestyle competition, a new gymnastic approach to the sport, was introduced, followed by long-distance racing in 1976. Both one-design class racing (where sailors compete on identical equipment) and open class racing (where sailors compete on different brands) have flourished.

With the rapid growth of the sport, a number of problems arose relating to access and rights to the waterways, legal jurisdiction and insurance. Partially for these reasons and partially because of the phenomenal growth of the sport in Europe, the International Yacht Racing Union (the international federation for the sport of yachting) decided that sailboards were yachts and that they should become part of the sailing community.

In 1978 the IYRU established a boardsailing committee to help frame international legislation to protect the rights of the boardsailor. In 1980 it granted "international status" to the Windsurfer® and Windglider® and proposed that the yachting part of the Olympic Games be expanded to include boardsailing as one of the events. Its proposal was accepted, and a boardsailing event and special exhibition were held at the 1984 Los Angeles Games.

The history of boardsailing is still new. No other water sport has developed so rapidly over a period of less than fifteen years. We invite you to become a part of it.

Meeting new friends at a regatta.

CHAPTER 1

Basic Sailing Theory

What do you know about the wind? Can you point out its direction and estimate its strength? If your answer is yes, you are well on your way to a successful first attempt at boardsailing. If you are uncertain, no matter; it's easy to learn about the wind.

Let's assume that you are on the shore of a lake or ocean, gazing out over the water and contemplating your first try at boardsailing. You have been asked to point out the direction of the wind. Here are some clues that will help you.

The first and most obvious clue is the waves that the wind is creating. Waves travel parallel to the wind direction and will give you a good idea of where the wind is coming from. If there are any birds on the beach, note the direction they face. A bird will always face directly into the wind to keep its feathers from ruffling and to prepare it for takeoff. Birds take off into the wind and land facing the wind. Look for a flag in the area. It will also give you an accurate reading of the wind's direction. The most intimate knowledge of the wind comes, of course, from feeling it on your body. Try to be aware of the movement of air over your skin.

Once you have pinpointed the source of the wind, you should give some thought to its strength. Knowing the wind's strength is important to a successful learning experience for a number of reasons.

Learning to boardsail is next to impossible unless the wind is light and fairly constant. Light winds don't generate much wave action, and relatively calm water is essential to good balance on the board. You will want your first attempt to be enjoyable and proper conditions are essential.

A glassy water surface indicates that there is no wind, and any thought of sailing in such conditions should be abandoned. A sailboard won't move without wind! If the wind is strong and the water is being whipped into large, frothy waves, again don't venture out for your first attempt. When whitecaps begin to appear with a regular frequency, the wind is approaching 15 knots and will overpower a novice sailor.

Gusty wind is a problem for the boardsailor because it doesn't provide the constant force required for good balance on the board. Often the wind will puff hard and overpower the sailor, die out suddenly or change direction. Being able to read these shifts and gusts prepares you for the changes of sail trim that you must make to stay in control. Here again, the visual effect of the wind on the water's surface is a key. Small ripples moving more rapidly than the regular motion of the larger waves and appearing as dark patches signal surges of wind. Paying close attention to these areas of "black water" will save you from some frustrating moments.

Relatively calm water is ideal for the beginner. The wind speed should set a flag to a lazy undulation and begin to ruffle your hair.

After you have learned to boardsail, you may want to be more precise in your measurement of the wind. An anemometer to measure the speed of the wind and a compass to determine its direction are useful. If you don't want to buy these instruments, a quick call to the local weather office will give you all the meteorological information that you will need to plan your sailing day.

Points of Sail

Because a sailboard is dependent on the wind for its mobility, it's handy to refer to where you are going (your point of sail) in relation to the wind direction. Although the following maneuvers and terms may sound complicated, with a little practice they will become second nature to you.

Sailing upwind, or toward the wind, is called **beating**. Because it is impossible to sail directly into the wind, a boardsailor must

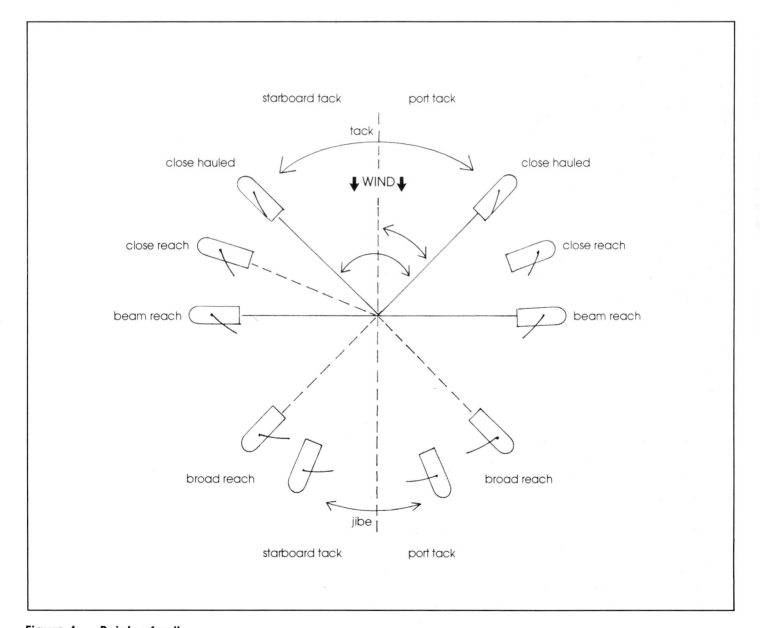

Figure 1.   Points of sail

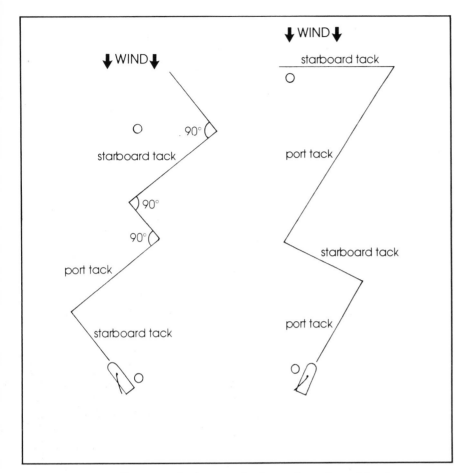

Figure 2.   Beating upwind on a starboard and port tack

approach an upwind destination by sailing a zigzag course toward it. The closest angle onto the wind that a sailboard can point is roughly 45°, and when sailing that course, a board is said to be sailing **close hauled**.

When sailing at any angle across the wind, a sailboard is said to be **reaching** or **on a reach**. A course 90° to the wind is called a **beam reach**. Sailing above that course (closer to the wind) is called a **close reach**. A course below a beam reach (away from the wind) is called a **broad reach**.

When the wind is coming from directly behind, the sailboard is on a **run** or **running with** (or **before**) **the wind**.

Preparing to tack.

16

The left side of a board when viewed from the stern is called the **port** side, while the right side is called the **starboard** side. When the wind is filling the left side of the sail, the board is said to be on a **port tack**. With the right side full, the board is on a **starboard tack**. A sailboard is always on a tack unless it is in the process of changing from one tack to the other. This change of tacks is called **tacking** when the board is moving upwind or **jibing** when the board is moving downwind.

Preparing to jibe.

Heading up refers to steering onto a course closer to the wind. When a sailboard points higher than 45° onto the wind, that is above being close hauled. The sail begins to flutter at the front, because it is impossible to trim it properly and still make way. The board stalls. When the hull is pointing due upwind, it is said to be **in irons** or **head to wind**. When the sail is trimmed to neither tack and flapping loosely, it is said to be **luffing**.

Bearing off refers to steering onto a course away from the wind. A sailboard can run before the wind on either tack and maintain the same course downwind.

Learning about the wind, feeling its power and coming to terms with it is an interesting experience. Try drawing the points of sail in the sand. Once you are familiar with them, you are ready to learn how to rig and launch your sailboard.

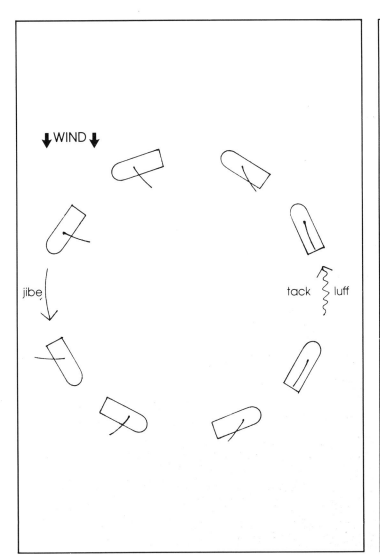

Figure 3.   Sailing in a counter-clockwise circle

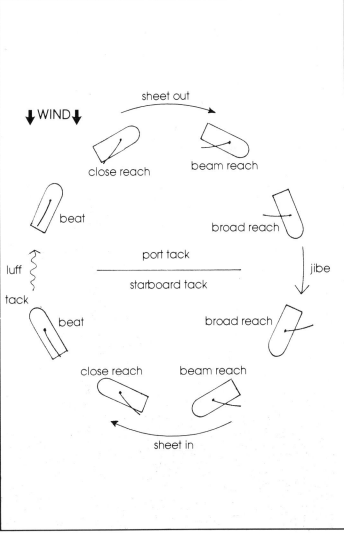

Figure 4.   Sailing in a clockwise circle

CHAPTER 2

Rigging and Launching

One of the attractions of boardsailing is the short length of time it takes to rig the craft. The freesail system has only three main parts: the rig, the hull and the daggerboard and skeg. You are the wires and lines that seem to clutter the deck of a conventional sailboat. You are also the tiller and rudder that are so obviously missing from the stern of the board. Rigging takes a matter of minutes and launching is as easy as entering the water for a swim.

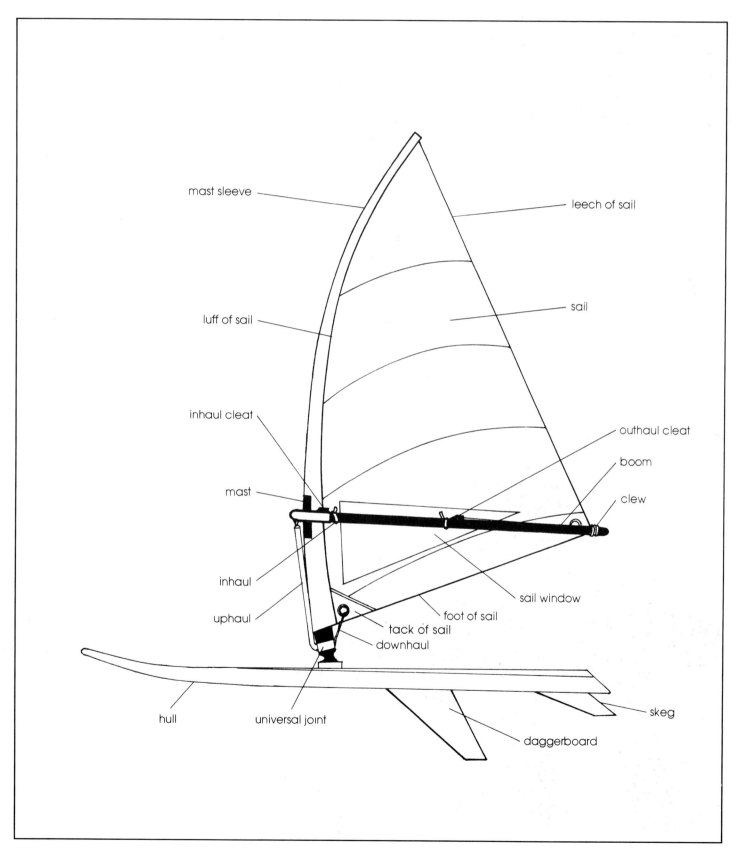

Figure 5.   Parts of a sailboard

Parts of a Sailboard

Rig This is your power source. The rig is comprised of the sail, mast and wishbone booms, which give the sail its shape and rigidity. It's attached to the hull by a device (a universal joint) that allows full rotation of the rig but does not support it in an upright position. The rig is pulled from the water to the upright position with the uphaul line.

Hull The hull is filled with foam and is unsinkable. It has a fitting to take the mast base, a slot amidships for the daggerboard, and fittings for a skeg or fin on the bottomside at the stern. The deck surface has a roughened texture for good traction.

Daggerboard and Skeg The daggerboard is the larger of the two and goes through the hull like a knife just aft of the mast base. It keeps the board from slipping sideways through the water and makes it possible to sail to windward. The size of the skeg or fin determines the ease with which the craft is steered. A small skeg gives less lateral resistance, which makes it easier to steer the board. A large skeg gives more lateral resistance, which provides greater directional stability and control at higher speeds.

Rigging

The many available freesail systems have component variations that make it difficult to describe specific rigging procedures for each type. The illustrated directions beginning on page 24 apply to all sailboards and will enable you to rig your board for maximum performance.

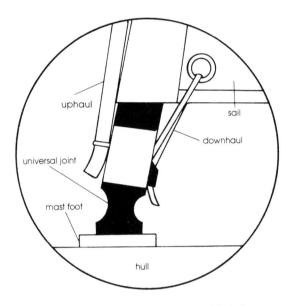

Figure 6.   Universal joint

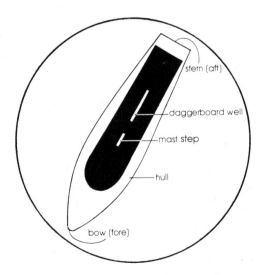

Figure 7.   Hull viewed from above

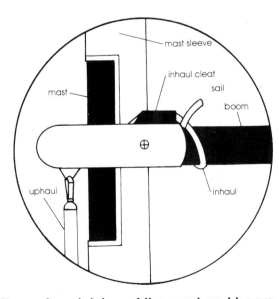

Figure 8.   Joining of the mast and boom

Fastening the outhaul line.

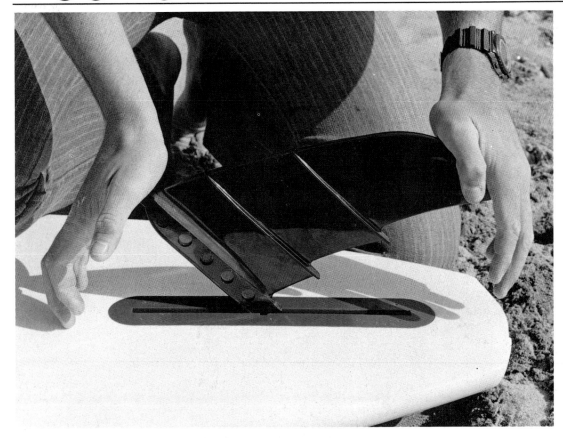

A common skeg attachment system uses a skeg box as shown here. To install, simply slide the skeg into the slot.

Tighten the screw to hold the skeg in place. Position the skeg forward in the slot for better maneuverability and aft in the slot for greater directional stability, enabling you to keep on course in high winds.

2. Inserting the Daggerboard

Most sailboards are equipped with a pivoting or a retractable daggerboard. Here Australian boardsailor John Buick inserts the daggerboard in a board prior to launching. He inserts it into the cassette from the deck side and rotates it back into its aft position.

3. Assembling the Rig

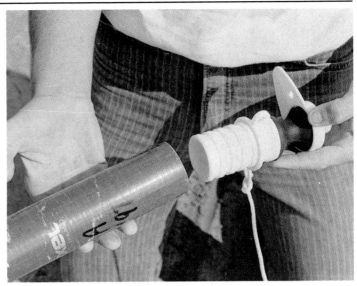

Attach the downhaul line to the mast base and insert the mast base into the mast. The downhaul line attaches the rig to the mast base and also controls the shape of the sail.

Lay the sail out on the ground and insert the mast into the sail sleeve.

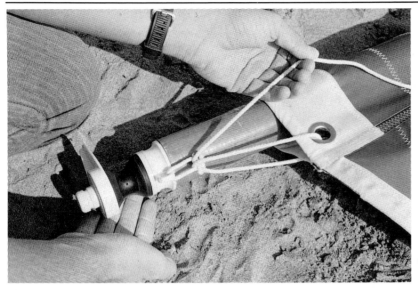

Feed the downhaul through the tack grommet on the sail and through the loop on the mast base. Tie or cleat the line loosely. (Final tensioning of the downhaul is the last step.)

If your sail has battens, the next step is to insert them into the batten pockets. Push the notched end of the batten into the pocket and tuck the round or flat end into the flap on the leech of the sail.

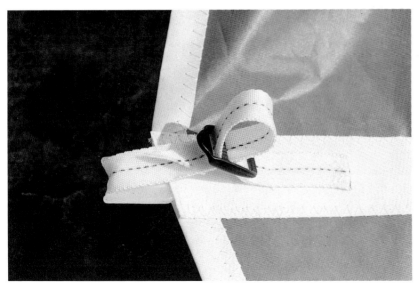

Some battens are held in place by a strap and buckle system. The notched end of the batten keeps the strap in place, preventing the batten from slipping out. This type of batten butts against the mast sleeve. The strap should be tensioned securely.

4. Attaching the Boom

The next step is to attach the inhaul line to the mast. This can be done with a variety of hitch knots or with a ball inhaul. Once tightened, the inhaul maintains the desired boom height, which is approximately at chin level. To determine where to attach the inhaul, stretch your arms wide along the mast from the mast base. Your height is roughly the same as the distance from fingertip to fingertip.

Ball inhaul.

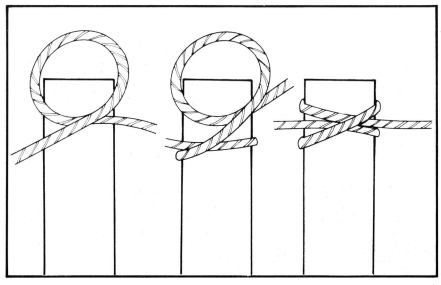

Clove-hitch knot.

Attach the uphaul line to the front end boom fitting. Lay the boom parallel to the mast and cleat (*this photograph*) or hook (*next photograph*) the inhaul line to the front end boom fitting. (Follow the manufacturer's assembly instructions.)

Swing the boom square to the mast. Pull the clew of the sail toward the opposite end of the boom and pass the outhaul line through the clew grommet on the sail and then through the rear end boom fitting. Tension it appropriately for the wind conditions and cleat it. In strong winds the sail should be as flat as possible, so pull the clew right out to the boom end. In light winds the outhaul can be slackened a bit to give the sail a fuller shape.

The final step in tuning the sail is tensioning the downhaul line. Horizontal wrinkles in the sail can be flattened with downhaul tension. Vertical wrinkles can be removed with more outhaul tension. The downhaul should be pulled very tightly for high wind conditions and snugly for light wind conditions.

5. Attaching the Rig to the Board

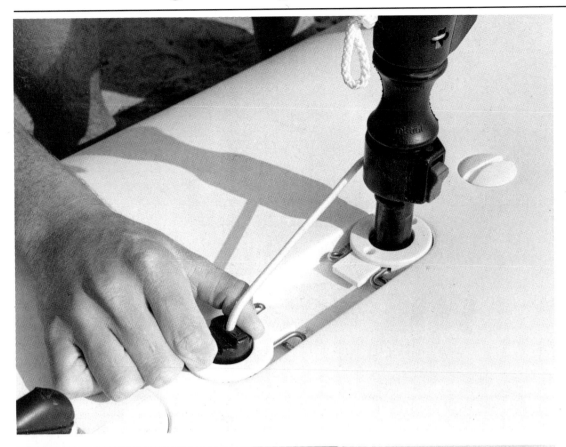

Lay the rig downwind of the board and insert the mast base into the forward mast step. Secure it with the locking mechanism. On some sailboards the mast base is attached to a sliding mast track.

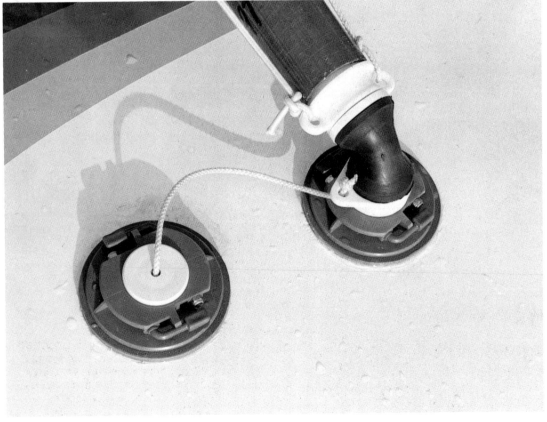

Lock the safety retention line into the aft step.

When the rig is attached to the board, hoist the sail, trim it to the wind, and check that all the lines are tensioned properly and the sail has no wrinkles.

Launching

Lift the rig with your fore hand.

Pick up the stern of the board with your aft hand.

Push the board into the water until the water is deep enough so that the skeg won't hit bottom.

Drop the hull and place your hands on the boom.

Step up onto the board, rake the sail forward and sail off. Once you are in deep enough water, rotate the daggerboard with one foot to the appropriate setting: down vertically for light wind or aft (or retracted) for high wind.

Alternate Launch

On a rocky beach or one covered with seashells, the bottom of the board can be scratched if it is pushed into the water. Hoist the rig and pick up the complete unit.

Carry the sailboard into the water.

Drop the board and sail off.

Getting Under Way

To get under way, the sailor stands on the hull straddling the mast, pulls the sail up with the uphaul line, positions the rig in front of him or her, grasps the boom and trims the sail onto the wind. The sailboard is steered by raking or leaning the sail toward the bow of the board to bear off the wind or toward the stern to bring the board up into the wind. How quickly you are able to learn these maneuvers depends on several factors. By following the five basic steps outlined in this chapter and by trying to be sensitive to the response of the board, you should have a successful first attempt with a minimum of falls. Choosing the right equipment, weather conditions and location are also important.

Equipment

A number of equipment options make learning much easier. A light rig is easiest to use. A wide hull gives greater stability and more buoyancy than a narrow one. It will help you maintain your balance and stay dry. Most sailboards are sold with a standard sail, approximately 60 ft² (5.5 m²) in area. However, a smaller sail is often better for the beginner. The one you choose should match your body size and ability to the wind strength (see page 38). Many boardsailing schools have a full range of sails to permit instruction in a number of different weather conditions.

As your confidence grows and your skills develop, you will move on to faster hulls and larger, more powerful sails (see Chapter 5).

Dry Land Exercises

The most important stage of the learning experience is what is done on land. A half hour of simulation on land equals two hours on the water. Learn to maneuver and balance the rig with the aid of a boardsailing school's simulator or simply stand on the hull on

Jinny Ladner, four-time Canadian women's champion, demonstrates how to practice on dry land.

the ground. (Be sure to dig a hole in the sand for the skeg or remove it.) Simulate sailing on both tacks and practice the rig movements of bearing off and heading up.

Weather Conditions and Location

Choose the day for your first try very carefully. Look for flat water conditions and very light winds. A consistent onshore wind (blowing from the water to the land) is reliable and will not push you offshore before you are ready.

Be sure to wear proper clothing for the air and water temperatures (see Chapter 12). Being cold immediately puts a damper on one's enthusiasm, concentration and endurance. A wetsuit will keep you warm and deck shoes or running shoes will protect your feet if you are sailing in rocky, shallow water. A life jacket is also mandatory and in some countries required by law.

The best place to introduce yourself to boardsailing is a secluded spot away from powerboat traffic. Leave yourself lots of room to make those inevitable first mistakes and try not to be frustrated by a few falls.

The five steps for getting under way on the following pages are intended for your first try on water; however, they should be practiced on land first. If an instructor is not available, have a friend read these steps to you to guide your progress.

Sail Choice for Beginners					
	Sailor's Weight				
	50-100 lb (20-45 kg)	**100-125 lb (45-55 kg)**	**125-150 lb (55-65 kg)**	**150-175 lb (65-75 kg)**	**175+ lb (75+ kg)**
Wind Strength in Knots	**Sail Area (Approximate)**				
2-5	45 ft² (4.0 m²)	50 ft² (4.5 m²)	50 ft² (4.5 m²)	60 ft² (5.5 m²)	65 ft² (6.0 m²)
5-10	45 ft² (4.0 m²)	50 ft² (4.5 m²)	50 ft² (4.5 m²)	50 ft² (4.5 m²)	60 ft² (5.5 m²)
10-15	30 ft² (2.5 m²)	40 ft² (3.5 m²)	45 ft² (4.0 m²)	50 ft² (4.5 m²)	50 ft² (4.5 m²)
15-20	not advisable	40 ft² (3.5 m²)	40 ft² (3.5 m²)	45 ft² (4.0 m²)	50 ft² (4.5 m²)
over 20	not advisable	not advisable	40 ft² (3.5 m²)	40 ft² (3.5 m²)	45 ft² (4.0 m²)

The Five Steps for Getting Under Way

1. Squaring Up

Stand on the hull with your feet on either side of the mast base, and grasp the uphaul line with both hands, squaring the hull to the mast. Begin to hoist the rig by pulling hand over hand on the uphaul, until the mast is upright enough for the clew of the boom to swing freely. Allow the sail to luff. The board will drift slowly with the wind. Hold the rig in front of you. The mast should be perpendicular to the board. This will keep the hull square to the wind.

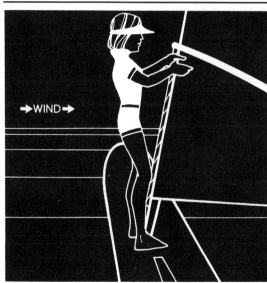

Take hold of the rig by the mast with fairly straight arms, back and legs, and find a comfortable point of balance.

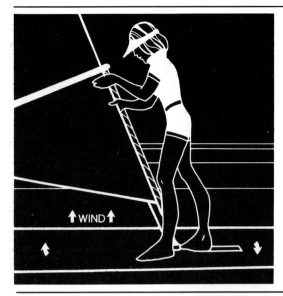

Now try turning the hull by leaning the sail forward toward the bow of the board.

Now try turning the hull by leaning the sail aft (toward the stern of the board).

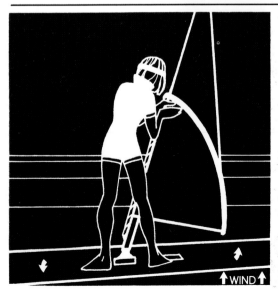

The next step is to turn the hull full circle. Keep the sail luffing and the wind at your back. Stand with your feet close to the mast base and walk the hull around. Once the rotation is complete, stop the board by holding the rig in a neutral central position and lean the sail toward the opposite end of the board, initiating a turn in the opposite direction.

Bringing the hull full circle, stopping it again in the square position with the rig leaning toward the bow, **jibes** the board around — the bow passes under the sail. Leaning the rig toward the stern **tacks** the board around — the stern passes under the sail. You are now able to position the board in the square position and ready to get under way.

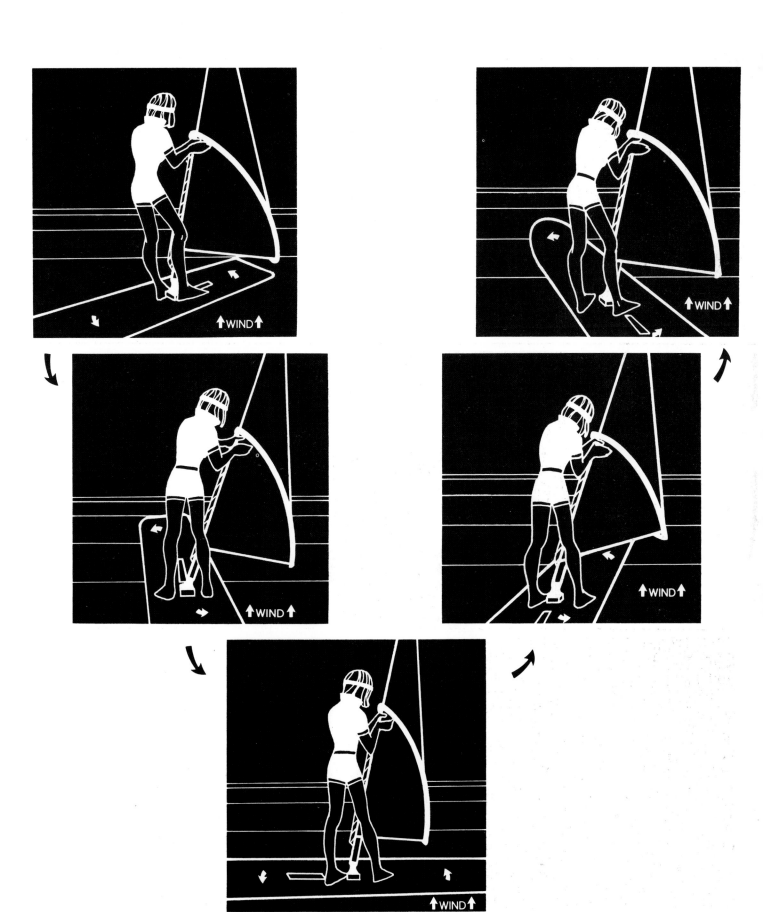

2. Sighting a Heading

Look around the horizon for a buoy on the water or a building on land to use as a potential heading. By selecting a number of points of reference around you, you are better prepared to keep your bearings. Check the water behind you for gusts and get comfortable without having to look at the hull or sail. Remember, you have to be able to see where you are going!

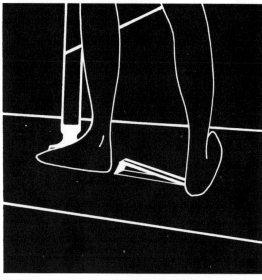

With the fore hand on the mast, move your feet so that they straddle the daggerboard, keeping the fore foot close to the mast base and pointing toward the bow.

Pull the sail across in front of you by rotating your hips and shoulders toward the bow. You should now be sighting your chosen heading. Lean the sail fore or aft to maintain that heading and keep the board square.

3. Grasping the Boom

Place your aft hand on the boom almost 3 ft (1 m) back from the mast. Keep the sail luffing and the hull square.

Quickly move your fore hand from the mast to a position 1 ft (30 cm) back from the mast, again keeping the board square and the sail luffing.

4. Trimming the Sail

Now simultaneously push the mast toward the bow of the board with the fore hand as you pull in with the aft hand to bring the sail across the wind and more in line with the hull. This is a combined move of raking the sail forward and sheeting in. Try to keep the pull balanced on both arms.

5. Getting Under Way

Lean back against the increasing pull of the sail by bending your aft leg and push the hull forward with your straight fore leg. Both arms should be almost fully extended for proper balance. Repeat the five steps a number of times before sailing too far. Turn the board around and do it again on the opposite tack until you are familiar and comfortable with getting under way on both tacks.

Coming Ashore

Watch the depth of the water as you approach the shore. Jump off before the skeg or daggerboard hits bottom.

Holding the mast with one hand and the boom with the other, push the board to shore.

Still holding the mast with one hand, lift the stern of the board with the other and push the sailboard up onto the beach.

Solving Problems

If problems, such as a gust hitting the sail, are experienced at any stage, simply release the boom with the aft hand, hold onto the boom with the fore hand and come back into the initial square position to start again. Try to avoid dropping the sail. Hoisting it a number of times from the water can be tiring. However, if you do lose control, the sailboard will come to a halt immediately as soon as the sail is dropped and hits the water. If you fall from the hull, simply swim back to it, climb on and start again.

Should the wind die out or become too strong, sit down on the hull, remove the mast from its fitting, uncleat the outhaul line and furl the sail around the mast. Swing the booms parallel to the mast and secure them with the outhaul. Lay this package on the hull, lie on it and paddle ashore using your hands. Remember, it takes patience to learn boardsailing. If you start to feel tired, don't feel embarrassed about furling the sail and paddling in.

After you have mastered the five basic steps, you are well on your way to becoming a proficient boardsailor.

CHAPTER 4
Basic Sailing

The following basic maneuvers will enable you to sail on all possible points of sail in light wind. With several hours of practice, your confidence will grow and you will want to test your skills in higher winds.

Steering

The sailboard is steered by tilting the rig either toward the bow or toward the stern. Raking the sail forward (toward the bow) heads the boat downwind (first diagram). Raking the sail aft (toward the stern) turns the boat upwind (second diagram). Raking the sail is accomplished by simple arm movements. When the rig is raked forward, the fore arm is straight and the aft arm is bent. When the rig is raked aft, the fore arm is bent and the aft arm is straight. When steering upwind, avoid pulling (sheeting) the sail in or across the wind too far, as this will stall the sail.

Maintaining Course

Once the board has been brought onto the desired course, bring the rig to a neutral or central position which holds the board on that course. By keeping an eye on your heading, you will automatically make the adjustments of sail trim. Rake it forward slightly if the board points above your heading, or rake it aft slightly if the board drops below your heading.

Sailing Downwind

Sailing downward or running with the wind is probably the trickiest point of sail. It requires a slightly different stance and an odd positioning of the rig.

While sailing on a beam reach, tilt the rig forward to bear off the wind until the hull is pointing almost straight downwind.

At this point the sail will become perpendicular to the hull and the wind. Your feet will be stradding the center line of the hull on either side or slightly aft of the daggerboard well and pointing toward the bow of the board. The boom will be horizontal and in front of you.

Tacking

Being on a tack is sailing a constant course. Tacking is bringing the board around onto a new course by turning the hull up into the wind, stepping around the front of the mast to the opposite side of the sail and bearing off onto the new course.

While sailing on a beam reach, rake the rig aft to start the hull turning up into the wind.

As the hull approaches head to wind, release your aft hand from the boom and grasp the mast.

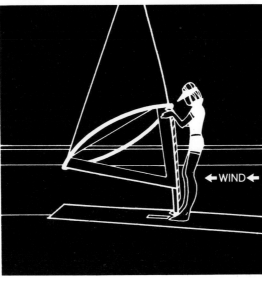

Step around to the front of the mast and square the board up. Proceed with the five steps for getting under way.

ABOVE It's always a good
idea to check your rig
before going for a sail.

OPPOSITE Sailing with a friend
in light winds.

Jibing

Jibing is steering the board around onto a new course by turning the hull downwind and around onto the new course.

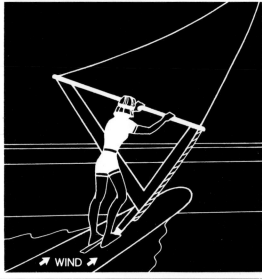

While sailing on a beam reach, rake the rig forward until the hull is heading straight downwind.

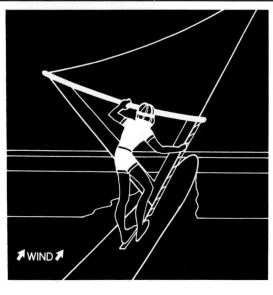

Release your fore hand from the boom and grasp the mast.

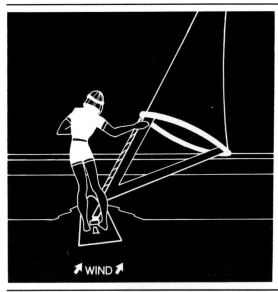

At this point, release your aft hand from the boom allowing the clew of the sail to swing around to the opposite side of the hull.

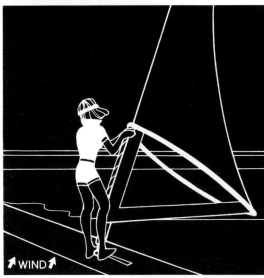

Grasp the mast with both hands as the board continues its rotation.

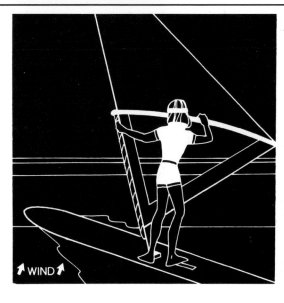

Square up and proceed with the five steps for getting under way.

CHAPTER 5

High Wind Boardsailing

Boardsailing in high wind is the most exciting form of sailing. The sailor is as free as the wind itself, fully in control and able to fly across the waves.

As the wind and boardspeed increase, there are a few small alterations that should be made to the sailboard. The simplest change is to flatten the sail by pulling it out tightly with the outhaul. If the wind is very strong, you will find it easier to use a smaller sail (see page 69). A full-sized daggerboard will also cause a control problem; the hull will roll up onto its rails. Reducing the daggerboard area by pulling it up halfway or rotating it up and back in the hull will partially alleviate this problem. Or you can use a specially designed high wind daggerboard, which makes the board very responsive, except when sailing upwind. The board can't point as high into the wind with the smaller daggerboard. Caution must therefore be used when a powerful offshore wind is blowing.

The maneuvers that are used in high wind sailing are basically the same as those used in light wind sailing. The difference is that the sail develops more power from a stronger wind and you are able to execute these moves more quickly. The quicker the move is made, the sooner you will gain balance on the rig and be under way.

Getting under way in a strong wind requires good concentration, a little more muscle and faster movements. The difficulty lies in having the confidence to lean back against the stronger pull of the sail and to tilt the rig forward far enough to bear off as you gain way. It's advisable to practice this move on land to avoid falling repeatedly when you are on the water. As you become proficient with the moves required, you will find the proper balance points and be ready to try it on the water.

You will find when you sail in high winds that the hull becomes less stable with the increased wave action and you become more dependent on the sail to keep you out of the water. The hands must move aft slightly on the booms to keep the rig balanced. If the hull tends to head upwind, tilt the rig forward toward the bow as you sheet in. Think of your aft hand as an accelerator. The more you sheet in, the faster you go because of the increased power. Sheeting out spills wind from your sail and reduces the power.

Canadian boardsailor
François Vinet moving fast
on a sportboard.

Experts often use fully battened sails in high winds.

Getting Under Way in High Winds

Hold the boom with both hands and allow the sail to luff.

↖ WIND ↖

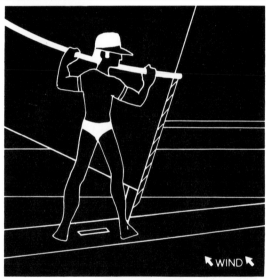

Rake the rig forward and across the hull. Keep the sail luffing.

↖ WIND ↖

↓ WIND ↓

Bend both knees and sit back as you sheet in with the aft hand. Push hard on the fore foot to bear off the wind.

WIND

Move your hands aft on the booms and move your feet aft on the board after you are under way.

ABOVE A game of high-speed chase on funboards.

LEFT Leaning back against the pull of the sail in a strong wind.

Many sailors use recreational boards to commute at yacht clubs.

Fast Tack

A fast tack in high wind is essentially the same as a tack done in light wind except that it is done much more quickly and the squaring-up step is omitted. To counter the greater pull of the sail in stronger winds, bend your legs to lower your center of gravity.

While sailing on a beam reach, rake the rig aft quickly, at the same time moving your aft foot farther toward the stern of the hull. Under full sail power, the hull rounds up very quickly into the wind.

Move sharply around the front of the mast, releasing the aft hand.

With the new fore hand, grasp the mast and pull it immediately across in front of you without bringing the hull around to the square position.

Place the aft hand 3 ft (1 m) back on the boom. Shift your fore hand from the mast onto the boom, 1 ft (30 cm) aft of the mast.

Fall back against the pull of the sail, pushing the bow around onto the desired heading with the fore foot. Move your feet farther aft as the boat picks up speed. Moving the feet corresponds to moving the hands for balance and allows you to sail much faster.

ABOVE Short radical fun-
boards with high tech sails
are the fastest sailboards in
winds over 20 knots.

LEFT Sailing inside the reef
on a recreational sailboard.

A downwind jibe.

Fast Jibe

Again, the fast jibe is done essentially the same way as a jibe in light wind, but under full sail power is done more quickly.

While sailing on a beam reach, rake the rig forward sharply and place your front foot forward slightly, causing the board to bear off. Be prepared to spill wind from your sail at this point by sheeting out. A sudden buildup of power on the sail will pull you forward and off-balance.

As the hull moves around downwind, pivot your aft foot and place your fore foot back toward the stern of the hull.

Pull hard on the front end of the boom and drive the stern around.

Grasp the mast with the fore hand and release the aft hand from the boom, letting the wind flip the clew of the sail around to the opposite side of the hull.

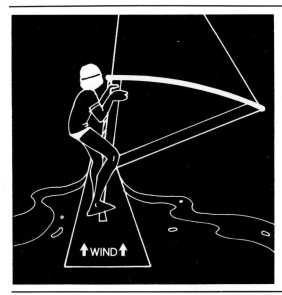

Place your aft hand on the mast and with both hands pull the sail across in front of you.

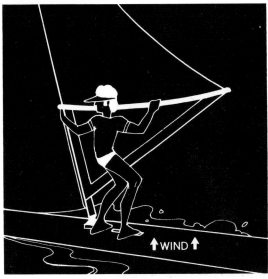

Quickly place the aft hand on the boom about 3 ft (1 m) from the mast.

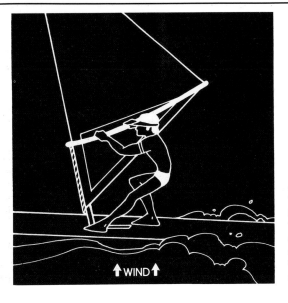

Shift your fore hand from the mast to the boom and sheet in, continuing to rake the rig aft until the hull comes around onto the desired heading. Move your feet ahead slightly as you get under way.

67

Water Start

When sailing in strong winds, you will sometimes find yourself in the water on the windward side with your feet still on the hull and the sail a few inches above the water's surface. Recovery from this position is possible without having to climb back onto the hull and without having to hoist the sail.

Push up with the fore hand to raise the mast and sail higher into the wind, sheet in a bit to build power in the sail and rake the rig forward to keep the hull square. Spread your feet wide over the daggerboard area to keep the hull drifting sideways. When a strong gust hits the sail, sheet in to develop enough power to lift you from the water. Rake the rig forward and set your new course.

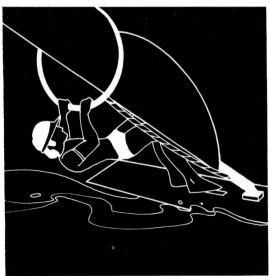

Sail Choice for Advanced Sailors

Wind Strength in Knots	Sailor's Weight				
	50-100 lb (20-45 kg)	100-125 lb (45-55 kg)	125-150 lb (55-65 kg)	150-175 lb (65-75 kg)	175+ lb (75+ kg)
	Sail Area (Approximate)				
2-10	50 ft² (4.5 m²)	60 ft² (5.5 m²)	65 ft² (6.0 m²)	65 ft² (6.0 m²)	65 ft² (6.0 m²)
10-20	30 ft² (2.5 m²)	50 ft² (4.5 m²)	60 ft² (5.5 m²)	60 ft² (5.5 m²)	65 ft² (6.0 m²)
20-25	not advisable	45 ft² (4.0 m²)	50 ft² (4.5 m²)	60 ft² (5.5 m²)	60 ft² (5.5 m²)
25-30	not advisable	not advisable	45 ft² (4.0 m²)	50 ft² (4.5 m²)	60 ft² (5.5 m²)
over 30	not advisable	not advisable	40 ft² (3.5 m²)	45 ft² (4.0 m²)	50 ft² (4.5 m²)

Flare

Also known as a "wheelie," the flare is a good way to slow the hull quickly and initiate a fast jibe. This maneuver is spectacular when done in a strong wind.

From a beam reach, tilt the rig forward, bear off and strive for top speed. As the hull comes into line with the wind, kick the hull forward by stepping quickly toward the stern.

Pull the boom down hard toward you as the bow rises. Then ease your pull on the boom and step forward. The hull will flatten out and continue downwind. Hold the rig in toward you until the hull stops. Leaning the rig laterally at this point initiates a fast tack or jibe. Step forward quickly on the hull once it has stopped.

Boardsailing with a Harness

Once you have mastered the basics and find yourself limited by burning hands and forearms, you are ready for sailing with a harness. The harness is a jacket-like device worn by the boardsailor, which attaches him or her to the rig. The sailor's body weight, used to counter the pull of the sail, is 75 percent supported by the harness, leaving the hands and arms free to make the continuous adjustments in sail trim.

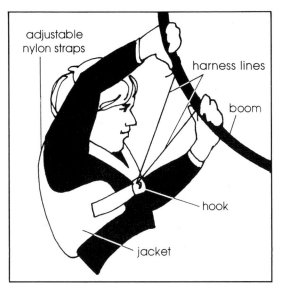

Figure 9.   Harness

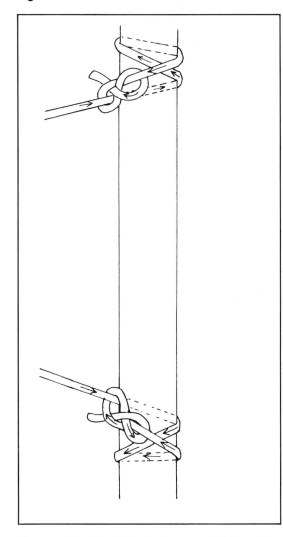

Figure 10. Half-hitch figure-eight knots

Parts of a Harness

The harness consists of the jacket that you wear and two lines, one attached to each boom.

The harness jacket is a foam-padded nylon or dacron jacket designed to support the upper body comfortably. Many harnesses are also PFDs (personal flotation devices). Nylon webbing straps over the shoulders adjust the height of the harness hook, which hooks onto the harness lines. Another strap across the chest closes the jacket through the hook with a quick release clip. The hook can be positioned pointing up or down.

The harness lines are attached to the booms using simple half-hitch/figure-eight knots or boom straps. The straps offer less interference to hand movement along the booms.

Setting Up the Harness

After you have rigged your sail, pick it up on land and trim it to the wind. This works well in a location with good exposure to steady wind.

When your hands have balanced the pull of the sail on the boom, you will have a good indication of where the harness lines should be tied. The ends of the lines should be attached just inside the hand positions. This will create a loop roughly 20 in (50 cm) long. The length of the harness lines will depend on your arm length and personal preference. Experimentation will determine the best position for a given wind condition. The basic rule to follow is: the higher the wind, the farther back the lines are placed from the mast. In an extremely high wind, the front end of a line will be up to 30 in (75 cm) from the mast.

When tying the lines on the booms, make sure that the knots or straps are tight and will maintain their positions. The half-hitch/figure-eight knot when tied correctly allows easy adjustment while sailing. Simply push up on the knots with the thumbs to loosen the hitches and slide the loops along to the desired position. Hook in, and your body weight cinches the knots. Straps tend to hold their positions very well once they are tightened.

Adjusting the Harness

Most harnesses allow hook height adjustments to be made by varying the length of the shoulder straps. The hook should sit between or slightly below the pectoral muscles.

The quick release closure makes it possible to adjust the harness to accommodate the added bulk of a wetsuit. A snug fit, which restricts breathing and movement, is not desirable, nor should the hook hang loosely, as this makes hooking in difficult.

When tying the booms to the mast, ensure that shoulder height is maintained. This position allows for the easiest hooking in and out.

Use of the Harness

Being hooked to your rig takes some getting used to, and initial attempts at sailing with a harness can be unnerving. As in learning anything new on your sailboard, first tries should be made in light onshore winds with your rig on dry ground.

Once your booms are rigged with the harness lines, pick up your rig and trim it to the wind to simulate a sailing situation.

With the Hook Down   Pull the boom toward you and down while raising your upper body as high as possible. This positions the hook above the harness line ready to hook in. You hook onto the line by lifting up on the boom and lowering your body. Extend your arms slowly until your body weight is countering the pull of the sail. Slide the boom either forward or backward until an evenly balanced pull is felt on the harness.

To unhook, pull the boom toward you and down. The line will drop from the hook. Extend your arms again and you will be sailing under manual power. Repeat this procedure until you can do it without having to look down at the line.

With the Hook Up   Pull the boom toward you and up, while bending your legs slightly. This will position the line above the upturned hook. Stand erect and lower the boom. The line will fall into the hook. Extend your arms slowly until your body weight counters the pull of the sail and slide the boom forward or backward until the rig is balanced.

To unhook, pull the boom toward you and up as you bend slightly at the knee. A more conscious effort is required to unhook with the hook up, and the sailor should be well acquainted with the procedure before trying it on the water.

The advantages of the hook up position are twofold: accidental hooking in is less likely and the loop stays in the hook while sail trim adjustments are being made.

Once you have familiarized yourself with hooking in and out on land, you are ready to try harness sailing on the water. Best results will be achieved in a light wind on nearly flat water. First attempts on the water should be made while sailing upwind.

Sailing downwind with the harness unhooked.

Tips

If the pull on your arms is decidedly one-sided, move the line in that direction. That is, if you have to pull hard on the fore hand to keep yourself balanced, the line is probably too far back on the boom. Moving the line forward a few inches by readjusting the position of the knot or strap will bring you into balance.

Learning to use a harness is easier if the line is positioned slightly forward of the central position of the boom. A line placed this way will make it easier to sheet out by spilling wind from the sail.

Points of Sail While Using the Harness

The harness is used to best advantage while sailing upwind. The strain on the arms is lessened dramatically. Race your friends to a far shore and back or take a lunch in a pack attached to your harness and go even farther afield.

The sailor should not be hooked in while running downwind because strain is minimal on this heading. However, sometimes the hook will snag on the line and throw the sailor off-balance. To avoid hooking in while running downwind, simply flip the line over the boom.

Using the Harness in Strong Winds

As your skill improves, you will be ready to try sailing with your harness in stronger winds. Bearing off onto a reach in high winds gives you the feeling of being instantly accelerated to near wind speed — very exciting in 25 knots, but be careful of the "launch."

Getting launched from the sailboard in strong, gusty winds is a somewhat unsettling experience, to say the least! If the rig is raked too far forward while you are hooked in, it becomes very difficult to counter the pull of the sail against the drag of the hull. The sailor is pulled off-balance, launching him over the bow of the board. The launch closely resembles pitch-poling in a catamaran sailboat or a good tumble on skis.

Continual use of the harness lines in strong winds will quickly wear out the line. Always inspect the line before going out on the water. Badly frayed lines should be replaced. By using an overlength line and varying the tail at either end, line life can be substantially prolonged.

CHAPTER 7

Competitive Boardsailing

Boardsailing has come a long way since its inception and so has the competitive side of the sport.

World champion Robby
Naish in his usual position
in a race — in the lead.

When boardsailing was in its infancy, only those people in the close circle around the manufacturer were involved in competitions. These took the form of "fun" races — out to a mark and back — and were indicative of the ability level of boardsailors at the time. As more people recognized the sport as an ideal recreational activity, small fleets of boardsailors began springing up all over North America, Europe, Australia and New Zealand.

The course chosen for competition was based on yacht racing's Olympic triangle course (see page 76). In Europe, championship racing quickly became a favorite weekend activity for thousands, with French, German, Italian and Dutch sailors leading the way. In the United States, some boardsailors soon tired of triangle racing and became experts in the alternative events — long-distance and slalom racing, and particularly the freestyle events.

At the same time, numerous new European manufacturers were getting involved in the industry, and "open class" racing began to emerge. It became the proving ground for the latest designs, with each new board being touted as the fastest. While these developments took place in Europe, a group of innovative boardsailors in Hawaii began taking the sport in the direction of surfing, moving to shorter, more maneuverable boards suited to the demanding winds and waves of the Pacific Ocean. Open "construction class" racing became the drawing card for individuals with ideas of their own to test in competition. In fact, most of the technical advances in modern sailboards have come from this direction. Soon surf sailing events were added to boardsailing competitions, and, most recently, a high-speed surf slalom competition.

Today boardsailing competition has come full circle. Small local "fun" competitions, with a strong emphasis on the social aspects of the sport, are now taking place in numerous countries. Regional events are drawing the best club sailors to well-organized competitions. Talented sailors from these events are then entering national and international events. Open class racing is strongest at the local/regional level with the emphasis on having fun and improving skills. At the world level, one-design racing is showing the greatest growth. Boards such as the BIC Wing, Mistral Superlight and Windsurfer® one design are all well-established brands with large class associations to administer their worldwide competition schedules.

At the apex of amateur boardsailing is the Olympic Games. At the 1984 Los Angeles Games, boardsailors from 38 countries competed in the yachting event, which consisted of seven individual races on Windgliders® through an elongated Olympic triangle course. Stephen van den Berg from the Netherlands won the gold medal, American Scott Steele the silver and New Zealander Bruce Kendall the bronze. A women's division is to be added in the near future. A two-day exhibition of boardsailing included three Windsurfer® class events: slalom, freestyle and long distance.

As in any sport with such mass appeal, there is now a professional circuit. Regional and national events for high-speed ''funboards'' offer substantial cash purses for boardsailors who compete in open construction class racing, surf sailing events and high-speed surf slalom events, culminating in the prestigious World Cup. The World Sailboard Manufacturers' Association (WSMA) Pool strongly supports a series of pro events with groups of top racers riding the various manufacturers' products for cash endorsements and large purses. World Cup events draw in excess of 150,000 spectators to windswept beaches, and in Europe, top racers' names are becoming household words.

Boardsailing competition is second to none. The following pages just might be your first step in becoming a Ken Winner, Robby Naish or Anick Graveline.

A Race with Your Friends

Before you and your friends head for the local regatta, you may want to practice first in your own race. The standard course, which has been adapted from sailboat racing, is the Olympic triangle course.

Olympic Triangle Course   On an Olympic triangle course, the sailor sails the three main points of sail: a beat, a reach and a run. The first leg of the course, called the weather leg, begins below the triangle course on a starting line situated between two marks placed square to the wind. (These marks can be old, spray-painted Javex bottles, painted inner tubes or buoy balls.) After the ten-minute starting sequence has been completed, the sailboards tack upwind to the windward or weather mark. The usual practice is to round the marks (without touching them) to port, that is, leaving them on the port side of the board.

The second leg of the course is called the starboard broad reach. The sailboards sail downwind on a broad reach to the reaching or jibing mark. Here the boards jibe around the mark, leaving it to port, and proceed on the third leg. The third leg is a port broad reach on the opposite tack toward the leeward mark, which is situated just above the start line.

Rounding the leeward mark, the boards head back upwind on the second beat, the fourth leg of the course. After rounding the windward mark for the second time, the fifth leg of the course is a

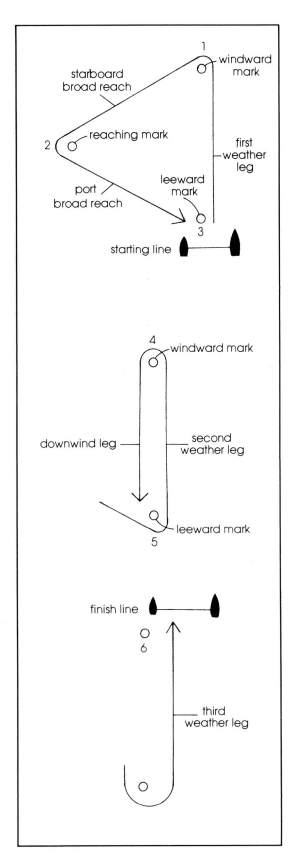

Figure 11.   Olympic triangle course

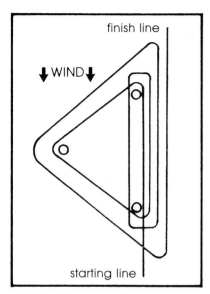

Figure 12. Course used in the 1984 Los Angeles Olympic Games

run straight downwind to the leeward mark, which again is rounded to port. The sixth leg is the final beat to the finish line, located upwind of the windward mark.

A board has finished the course as soon as the bow touches the line. It must cross the line and clear the finish area immediately to make way for following boards.

To simplify this course, the start/finish line can be one and the same, placed halfway between the windward and leeward marks. This also shortens the course by half of the first and last beats.

In most regattas, a committee boat is used by the judges, who give the starting sequence, watch for fouls, etc. However, a small group of boardsailors can avoid the need for a committee boat by using a rabbit start. In a rabbit start one board crosses in front of the other boards or the fleet on a starboard tack. The individual boards in the fleet start when the starter (rabbit) board passes them. The rabbit must jibe before sailing a course to the windward mark so that he doesn't have an advantage over the other boards.

Starting a Race There are a number of variations to the starting procedure. We will discuss a format that is useful for small regattas.

A line consisting of two marks set square to the wind comprises the start line of a sailing race. Enough room must be allowed between these marks to accommodate all the boards in the fleet. The race committee should be in a boat at the starboard end of the line, unless a rabbit start is being used.

In most sailing races, a ten-minute start sequence is used. For your race, however, a five-minute sequence will probably be sufficient to prepare the fleet for the start.

A watch is very helpful to guarantee a good start. At the precise moment when the start sequence begins, you should note the time. This ensures that you are physically in the right place and mentally prepared for the final signal. You can also time the committee and make sure that the starting sequence is being handled correctly. In large regattas, if a sailor finds that the starting sequence is incorrect, he or she has the right to protest to the race committee.

There are a number of sailing watches on the market. The most practical and economical are the lightweight, plastic-encased digital watches with a stopwatch feature. These are available at approximately one-fifth the price of specialized sailing watches.

After all the boards have arrived in the starting area, the race committee should simultaneously hoist a red flag and sound an audible signal (either a gunshot or a horn blast) to begin the five-minute countdown to the start. Sailors should set their watches at this signal. Four and one-half minutes into the sequence the red flag is dropped. On Go, the red flag is raised and the audible signal is given to start the race.

Any boards over the line early have their numbers called on a loudhailer and must round either end of the start line and start again or be disqualified. If too many boards are over early to call individual numbers, a general recall signal is sounded (three blasts) and the full five-minute sequence begins again.

Preparing for a Local Competition

When you feel you are ready to race in a local regatta, ask your dealer or club officials for details of regatta schedules and association membership forms. Dealers can be most helpful in getting you started.

Don't be worried about your level of expertise. Most regattas hold races for more advanced racers (the A fleet) and for beginning racers (the B fleet). Nor do you have to worry about your size or strength. Each competitor is usually placed in a weight class. Weight classes consist of lightweights and heavyweights. The cutoff points depend on the number of people in the regatta and the distribution of weight. There is sometimes a special class for women; however, if there aren't enough women competitors to form a fleet, they race with the men.

Where once athletic, longtime boardsailors dominated most events, conventional small boat sailors are now turning their talents to boardsailing competitions and are proving that brawn is not necessarily required to win a race. A knowledge of racing tactics and skillful board handling usually add up to a victory.

Rules   To compete successfully, the boardsailor should have a good understanding of the rules regulating sailboard racing. These regulations are designed to establish right of way of one board over another and to prevent collisions. Tactics, which are based on the rules, are obviously very important in racing. The better your knowledge of the regulations, the better your chances of winning a race.

The rules can be studied in the International Yacht Racing Union book or in a book on sailing tactics such as Eric Twiname's *The Rules Book*. As your racing experience grows, you will begin to understand the rules more fully and be able to recognize instances where they can be used to your advantage over other boards. Here are a few basic rules to help keep you out of trouble on your first race.

1. Port/Starboard Boards   When two boards on opposite tacks are approaching a common point, the starboard tack board has right of way. The port board must either give way and go behind, or tack onto starboard and keep clear.

Fighting for clean air while sailing to the reaching mark.

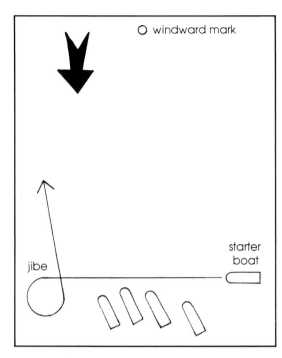

Figure 13. Rabbit start

2. Windward/Leeward When two boards on the same tack are overlapped, the leeward board has "luffing rights" over the windward board. The leeward board can head up, and the windward board must keep clear. When an overlapped windward board reaches a position where its daggerboard is even with the leeward board's mast, the sailor calls "mast abeam" and the leeward board loses its luffing rights. The overtaking board (windward here) must keep clear, however.

3. Room at Marks When two boards approach a mark, and the inside board has an overlap on the leading board at the moment that board's bow enters the two-board-length circle around the mark, the following board calls for "buoy room" and must be given ample room to round the mark.

4. Room to Pass Obstructions When two boards on the same tack approach an obstruction, the right of way board can't force the other board into that obstruction. The right of way board must waive those rights and allow the other to clear the obstruction.

5. Tacking and Jibing A board must keep clear of other boards while tacking or jibing. While the sail luffs during tacking or jibing, a board has no rights over others.

6. Ample Room and Opportunity If a board suddenly achieves right of way over another by tacking onto starboard or becoming the leeward board, the other board must be given ample room and opportunity to keep clear.

7. Touching a Mark Touching a mark is a foul. The mark must be re-rounded.

8. Penalties A board that fouls another can exonerate itself from that foul by doing a 720° turn as soon as possible after the infringement. The fouled board should notify the culprit of his intention to protest. A board has no rights while doing a 720°, or while re-rounding marks, including start line marks.

Board Handling Board-handling skills are very important in competition. You must be able to remain in control of your board in all situations and derive maximum power from the wind and water conditions. With the confidence gained through experience and practice, you will soon find yourself in first place at the windward mark.

To brush up your skills prior to a race, practice the basic maneuvers of tacking, jibing, sailing close hauled, and running downwind.

Sailing to Weather   Successful sailing close to the wind should also be practiced before a race. A skillful sailor will be able to show you just how high you can point.

Three things to keep in mind when racing upwind are:
1. Keep maximum power on the sail. This you sense through your hands. You will feel if the sail is pulling hard or not.
2. Point as high as possible into the wind. Keep your eye on the windward mark and tack on all wind shifts that are advantageous.
3. Maintain good board speed. Don't pinch or head too high up into the wind, to the point where you lose speed.

Racing Techniques   Proper technique is crucial to windward performance. Concentration is required to hold the board on the best angle of attack when approaching the windward mark.

In light wind, the rig should be held as upright as possible and trimmed closely to or over the hull's center line. By keeping the arms and legs locked, a tight link between sailor and board is established and slight wind increases will be transferred directly to board speed. Placing the feet as closely as comfort allows to the daggerboard area minimizes unwanted changes in direction.

As the windspeed increases, a number of changes in technique must be made. Balance is improved when hands and harness lines are moved aft slightly in an average wind or radically in a heavy wind. With the center of effort moving aft, the feet must also shift to a position just behind the daggerboard well. By placing the feet closer to the edge of the hull, it becomes easier to hold the board level. There is a tendency for the hull to rail up when driven hard, and it is advisable when this happens to reduce the daggerboard area by pulling the daggerboard halfway up in the well or retracting it slightly.

Locking in or keeping your body rigid can also turn gusts in high winds to your advantage. You must, however, be prepared to move quickly in response to shifts or lulls.

When tacking, try to maintain speed onto the new heading. Trim the sail as quickly as possible and avoid excessive bearing off while getting under way. Long tacks are advisable in light wind as tacking takes too much time, unless a shift in the wind makes a new tack advantageous. You have only so much wind to work with, so make the most of it.

The Competition

The Start   A good start is always essential but not necessarily easy to achieve. With fifty to one hundred boards on the start line, it takes no imagination to envision the chaos that often develops. To avoid being late at the start, familiarize yourself before the race with the starting procedures chosen by the race committee. Check in early at the committee boat and sail along the line to

Two sailors tack to the windward mark. One competitor has chosen a starboard tack and thé other a port tack.

establish your preferred starting position. Before the ten-minute signal, sail a couple of tacks toward the windward mark. If time permits, sail a leg of the course and with another board try opposite tacks to determine which side of the course is favored. All this information will be highly valuable in determining your tactics for the race.

Be near the committee boat when the start sequence is being counted down to allow for an accurate watch setting.

Once the start sequence has begun, check the line a second time to see if the initial start plan is still valid. Observing experienced sailors will definitely help. (Try following one in the race, being careful of course to keep out of his or her way. Start just behind where he starts, tack when he tacks and watch his reactions at each mark.)

Check the daggerboard for weeds and take a quick last-minute look at all fittings on the sailboard. They should be okay if you checked them on the beach.

On most starts the starboard end will be favored because the board closest to this mark has starboard tack right of way over all other boards. However, if the port end of the line is set more upwind than the starboard end, the port end becomes more advantageous. These areas are prone to chaos, though, and unless you have excellent board-handling abilities, should be

ABOVE Three sailors broad reach on a port tack.

LEFT In a surf slalom competition, Hawaiian Peter Cabrinha keeps the lead with a fast jibe.

The downwind leg of an Olympic triangle course.

avoided. An unnecessary fall with ten seconds to go loses friends and the race. In your first races try to start from a less crowded position, where you will have clean air (wind that is not affected by the movement of other boards) and fewer boards to contend with.

It is desirable to have some speed when crossing the line, but this is not always possible as most of the boards will be right on the starting line, leaving no gaps to power through when the gun goes off. Always try to be in the front row of boards because the dirty air from the sails upwind makes it difficult to gain way.

Rounding Marks   The variations of board positions and the rules that apply to each situation at a mark are seemingly endless.

Knowing the rules inside and out and being able to see their application instantly will help in a race; however, all that takes time and experience. In the meantime, a few simple points should be kept in mind.

Always come to the windward mark in a position that gives you the right of way. On courses where marks are rounded to port, get on a final starboard approach a good distance from the mark, aiming high of the mark to allow for wind shifts and any boards that acquire inside rights. By coming in a little above the mark, you can always bear off and gain extra speed while rounding. If the wind is strong enough to permit planing conditions on the reach, reduce your daggerboard area once you have rounded to allow better hull control. If balance is a problem on the reach or run, try kneeling down on one knee or both if the water is rough. This will prevent an unwanted fall.

Try to come around the reaching and leeward marks without slipping too far downwind. Come onto the mark wide, initiate the jibe early and pass as closely below the mark as possible. With a lot of boards following upwind, the air is not very clean and can cause a sloppy jibe. Be prepared to leave sufficient room for boards with overlap rights.

Finishing   Try to finish on the favored end of the line on a starboard tack. Once across the line, sail clear of the area before celebrating or bemoaning your result. This is a simple act of courtesy that will be appreciated by competitors and race committee alike.

Long-distance and Slalom Racing

In addition to Olympic triangle racing, you may want to try long-distance or slalom racing.

A long-distance course is 6 mi (10 km) or more in length. A variation of the Olympic triangle course, it often consists of an upwind leg, a downwind leg and two reaching legs.

The long-distance race is often started from a Le Mans start. All the competitors line up on the beach with their boards placed near or at the water's edge. At the sound of the gun, they run to their boards, hoist their sails and get under way. Just as in Olympic triangle racing, there are favored ends of the start line. When picking a starting position or area to place your board, take the same things into consideration that you would at the start of an Olympic triangle race—the direction of the wind, location of the first mark, etc.

There are a few points to keep in mind if you plan to race long distance. A harness is indispensable and you should learn how to use one. Endurance and the ability to maintain concentration over a long period of time are essential. To build up your strength for long-distance racing, go for long sails with your friends.

Slalom racing is similar to the dual slalom in snow skiing. The course consists of two lines of three buoys lined up opposite each other. Two competitors sail through the markers in a prescribed

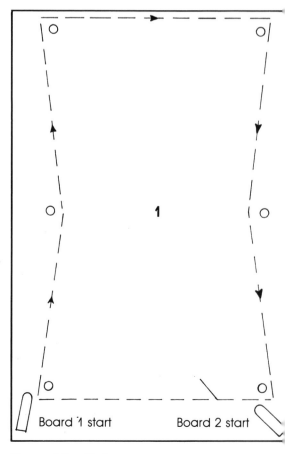

Figure 14.   Slalom course

fashion (see Figure 14) at the same time. Touching the marks is legal in slalom racing, but the sailing right of way rules apply. This type of race requires excellent jibing and tacking skills and tactical abilities.

If there is a violation of the method prescribed for going through the marks, a competitor is disqualified. Boardsailors who plan to slalom race should carefully study the proper way to go through the marks. People fail in slalom simply because they don't take the time to learn where they are supposed to go.

The starting sequence for a slalom race consists of three-minute warnings. A minute gun or horn blast is sounded and the sequence is audibly counted down from the thirty-second point. One boardsailor starts at the port end of the line and the other at the starboard end. The ends they start at are decided by the race committee. The person who finishes the slalom course first without any mistakes is the winner.

Both long-distance and slalom racing are included in most regattas along with Olympic triangle racing and freestyle competitions. The scores of a competitor who competes in all four events are combined to make up a cumulative score. The competitor with the lowest point score is declared the best all-round sailor at a regatta.

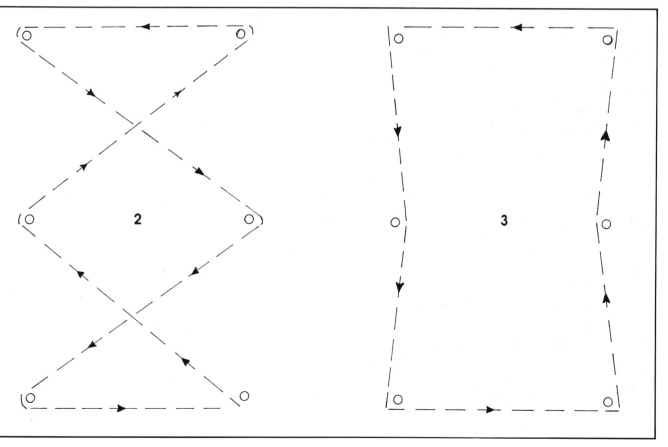

The course is followed by Board 1 in the diagram.
Board 2 sails a course that is the mirror image of Board 1's.

CHAPTER 8

Surf Sailing

Although not for everyone, surf sailing is certainly the most exciting and demanding aspect of boardsailing. The following instructions will give you the basics and some exercises to prepare you for your first try at surf sailing.

RIGHT Robby Naish surf sailing at Diamond Head in Hawaii.

OPPOSITE World Cup racer Ken Winner sails down the face of a wave.

A combination of sailing and surfing was what the originators of the sailboard had in mind when they conceived the sport. Sail power has obvious advantages over paddling between the waves with the hands. Instead of waiting as a surfer does for the perfect wave, the boardsailor is able to move through the surf to find the ideal place to catch the best ride. Every boardsailor has felt the acceleration caused by even the smallest waves on lakes. As the waves become larger, acceleration increases and an exhilarating ride is prolonged.

Before you attempt surf sailing, a few tips and notes of caution. Surf sailing is not recommended for the newcomer to the sport. Although the most exciting images of the sport in magazines and films are the wave riding and jumping shots from ocean locales, it must be remembered that the sailors riding in those conditions are very experienced. The conditions which allow this type of boardsailing are demanding and are, in most cases, dangerous. The amount of time required to become proficient at surf sailing will depend upon your proximity to ocean (or large lake) conditions, your ability and your free time to spend practicing the basics. It is also essential to be an expert swimmer.

A number of other factors are necessary for surf sailing: consistent, strong cross-shore winds, good waves, and the proper equipment.

How to Surf Sail

When you are proficient at boardsailing, the best way to introduce yourself to surf sailing is to find a location where the swells have no white water breaking on their crests and are about 3 ft (1 m) in height. Such conditions can be found on large lakes or some distance offshore in coastal locations.

On a beam reach, the sailor sights a wave, ahead and slightly upwind, and bears off down its face as it rises up under the hull. The sailor must be careful not to outrun the wind. Bearing off too quickly too far will move the hull ahead of the wind, causing the sail to become backwinded. This creates a balance problem. The sailor is usually knocked backward into the water by the sail. In higher wind, balance is more easily maintained.

The best conditions for surf sailing are found, of course, in coastal ocean locations. Not only are large waves a regular occurrence, but often the wind direction will vary from that of the wave travel. It is in such conditions that apparent wind (see below) can be used to the best advantage. The faster the craft accelerates down the wave, the stronger the apparent wind becomes. The result is a very fast ride.

Never attempt to surf sail in shorebreak, the waves breaking on the beach. This is extremely dangerous water. A hard fall can result in broken booms and mast, a torn sail and injuries to you.

Intermediate boardsailors should learn to surf sail in moderate winds and on small waves.

Apparent Wind

An interesting phenomenon takes place as a board's speed increases and approaches the speed of the wind. A new wind direction and velocity is created called apparent wind. One of the best explanations of apparent wind that we have found is in Stephen Colgate's book, *Colgate's Basic Sailing Theory*. He defines apparent wind as "the resultant wind derived from the wind produced by the boat moving through the air and the wind produced by nature — the 'true wind.'" He gives as an example a car heading north with a 10 mph (16 kph) easterly wind blowing. The wind will hit the right side of a passenger's face. As the car's speed increases, the passenger doesn't feel two different winds, one on the side of his face and one on the front, but a resultant wind coming from an angle forward of the true wind.

There are four basic thoughts to keep in mind when encountering apparent wind for the first time. The apparent wind always comes from a point forward of the true wind unless the true wind is astern or ahead. The second point is that the apparent wind lessens in velocity as the true wind comes aft. Third, a small change in true wind direction when it is well aft makes for a large change in apparent wind direction. Finally, when sailing on a beam reach or close hauled, the apparent wind has a higher speed than the true wind.

When bearing off in high wind, acceleration continues until the board is running almost dead downwind. Beyond this point, apparent wind decreases as acceleration is slowed by hull drag, until the sail is affected only by the true wind, which at this point comes from directly astern and is diminished by the speed that the board moves with the wind.

Apparent wind becomes a major factor in surf sailing. With the added acceleration of the wave, the apparent wind increases very quickly. It takes some time to get used to keeping the sail trimmed correctly to maintain balance.

Equipment

The types of sailboards used in surf sailing have undergone some some radical changes in the past few years, and continue to evolve on an almost daily basis.

For the most part, wave boards are in the 8–10 ft (2.4–3 m) range, with shapes and profiles identical to the boards used by surfers. The wave board's components consist of a strong mast attachment, which is usually a fin box mounted securely in the deck; four footstraps for control at high speed; and up to three fins or skegs for directional control.

The rigging used in surf conditions must also be durable enough to withstand repeated poundings by tons of water on sand or coral reef bottoms. Broken masts make up most of a surf sailor's equipment!

CHAPTER 9

Wave Jumping

"Air time" is a popular cry of freestyle skiers and is now being introduced to the sailing world. Pictures of sailboards suspended mysteriously above the water are appearing everywhere and explanations are in demand. How did they get up there? Like the skier who approaches a mogul on a ski slope, skis up it and shoots out into the air, the boardsailor approaches an oncoming wave, sails up its face and becomes airborne as the wave passes underneath.

ABOVE Robby Naish does a mule kick—kicking the board upside down to windward.

OPPOSITE Ken Winner about to touch down stern first.

The main requirements for wave jumping are lots of wind (at least 15 knots), footstraps on the hull and a good breaking offshore surf. In some locations, wind and wave directions are often not parallel. These areas offer the best jumping conditions because the angle formed between the wind and wave directions sometimes approaches 90° — ideal for the beam or broad reach needed to ascend a wave.

Wakes from large motorboats are also fun to jump and a cooperative driver can provide hours of enjoyment for the skilled and adventurous boardsailor. Unwary boat drivers are astounded when boardsailors approach their stern wakes and fly into the air. They are even more surprised at successful landings!

The best waves for jumping can be found on the Hawaiian islands of Oahu and Maui. Local conditions at Kailua, the North Shore and Diamond Head make it difficult to stay on the water. At Hookipa on Maui, there are perfect conditions for jumps on 5–15 ft (1.5–4.5 m) waves.

Footstraps

Sailors in Kailua, Hawaii, decided after many aborted leaps that a way was needed to keep themselves attached to their boards. The solution came in the form of neoprene-wrapped, nylon webbing straps. The straps resemble the fittings on the back of a slalom waterski. Two pairs are attached on either side of the daggerboard area and three more pairs are added toward the stern. This arrangement allows the sailor to maintain contact with the hull in a variety of sailing situations. First-time jumpers should place their feet loosely in the footstraps so that they can be released quickly and safely in the event of a fall.

A word of caution is needed here. Remember that wave jumping is for the competent boardsailor. Once you have gone through all the steps in this book and feel that you are highly proficient at them, then you might be ready for wave jumping. However, don't attempt it without instruction from experienced boardsailors. Ask them if you are ready for wave jumping and, most important of all, listen to their advice.

Making a Jump

The sailor must be very aware and confident when wave jumping. Dropping the rig in front of a breaking wave can result in damaged equipment. Jumping should be done only with strong, short boards that permit fast sailing and that withstand the impact of landing.

A breaking wave or swell diminishes in size from the curl, where the wave is cresting and the wave face is vertical, to a shallow slope of smooth water. Initial jumps should be attempted at the smaller end of the wave. Jumps will be low but chances of successful landings will be better. Once skill and confidence have been built, you can move along the wave to a position where you gain the greatest height from a vertical takeoff. Shallower slopes will give longer jumps with less altitude.

Pick your spot and sail with maximum speed on a beam or broad reach up the face of the wave. To set the sail horizontal for the best ''flight'' control, lean back as the board ascends the wave and prepare to rake the sail forward as much as you can. (In other words, try to bear off as far as possible at takeoff. This maintains forward motion and sets you up for a good landing.) As the crest is reached and the bow of your board comes up into the wind, pull up on the forward footstrap, lifting the windward rail up to present the hull flat onto the wind as it becomes airborne. This guarantees your takeoff. Allow full body extension for better balance in the air. Control is maintained by using the sail as a wing.

When the stern of the board begins to descend, feel for good balance on the sail. Keeping the sail full of air provides stability and softens your landing. Absorb the impact of landing with a slight flexing of the knees and lean back to pull the sail fully onto the wind. Sail to the next wave, jibe quickly and ride it in.

Robby Naish shows his great skill at wave jumping.

Looking down for a safe
landing.

Even small swells can be jumped.

CHAPTER 10

Freestyle Sailing

Light wind freestyle or trick sailing involves sail position variations and acrobatic body movements. With a stronger wind and more power on the sail, the hull can be put through a number of exciting figures.

LEFT American boardsailor Cort Larned sailing on the leeward side of the sail.

OPPOSITE European boardsailor Sigi Hoffman does a flip through the boom.

Most freestyle boardsailing has evolved through experimentation or accident, with no rules governing creativity. Many boardsailors try tricks to amuse themselves or an audience on the shore. The ten standard tricks on the following pages will help you start your own routine. In the process of learning them, you may even invent a few tricks of your own!

Here are several points to keep in mind when trick sailing. Tricks are easiest to learn in light wind but can with practice be done in strong wind. Rail rides and the body dip require more wind to be executed correctly. Lightweight booms and a tight rig are essential and, remember, always practice on dry land first.

1. Sailing on the Leeward Side of the Sail On a beam reach, move around the mast and stand on the leeward side, facing the sail and holding the boom. Turn your body 180°. You will be sailing in the same direction, but your back will be to the sail.

2. Sailing Clew First Jibe the board but don't flip the sail over onto the other tack. You will be sailing along with the hull pointing forward and the sail backward.

3. Sail 360 Sail on a beam reach. Push the clew of the sail to windward or leeward, then holding the same boom, walk around the mast base, rotating the sail a full 360°. This trick can also be done on the leeward side of the sail.

4. Hull 360 Sail on a beam reach. Turn the hull up into the wind and around a full 360° by holding the sail tilted aft. This turns the hull around rather than the sail. The sailor stays in a stationary position.

ABOVE Boardsailor Fraser Black sailing inside the boom.

BELOW LEFT Hull 360.

BELOW RIGHT Rail ride.

ABOVE Duck tack.

RIGHT A couple practice their freestyle routine.

A variation of sailing inside the boom.

5. Sailing Inside the Boom   Slide up inside the boom and rest your arms on top of it. Steer the hull in the same way as you would when sailing outside the boom.

6. Pirouette   Tip the sail to windward and luff it in a balanced position. Release the boom, pirouette by turning your body a full 360° and grab the same boom again when you have completed the pirouette.

7. Pirouette Tack   Pirouette once or twice around the front of the mast as you tack.

8. Rail Ride   Sail on a beam reach, flip the hull up on its edge and stand on it. Hook your fore foot under the windward rail and rest your shin on it. Then place your other foot on the top side of the rail. Sail frontward, backward and inside the booms.

9. Duck Tack   Hold the hull up into the wind. Instead of walking around the front of the mast to tack, duck under the sail and grab the opposite boom. Try a pirouette while ducking under the sail.

10. Body Dip   Sailing fast on a broad reach, drag your legs in the water while maintaining balance on the sail. Sheet out and drag your body under the water with your head above the surface. To regain your original position, sheet in and pull yourself up.

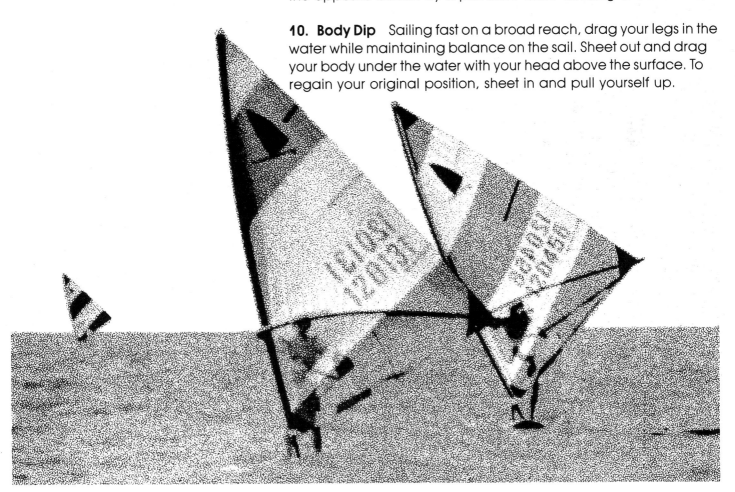

CHAPTER 11

Selecting Equipment

The wide selection of high-quality sailboards on the market today makes choosing the right board a difficult task for the newcomer to the sport. Products range from all-round recreational boards to the latest hi-tech funboards. Some are equipped with just the necessary components, some are loaded with the latest go-fast options, and prices range accordingly!

The Mistral Superlight and BIC Wing are recreational and one-design racing boards.

Choosing the Right Board

In selecting a sailboard, you should take an honest look at four important factors: 1. your athletic ability; 2. your leisure time; 3. your sailing environment; 4. price.

Athletic Ability How far are you likely to go in the pursuit of high-speed boardsailing? Anyone can experience the pleasure of boardsailing, but only a few dedicated athletes can handle the demands of Hawaiian surf sailing. When making a choice, select a sailboard that is well suited to your potential development and participation in the sport.

Your Leisure Time It takes more than just a few weekends during a summer to become proficient at sailing in strong winds, but not that long to learn the basics of sail handling and board control. If you're like the average sports-minded working person, you'll use your sailboard no more than fifteen times a season. If, on the other hand, you sail year-round in the tropics, your equipment selection criteria will be different, because you'll progress through the levels of proficiency much more quickly.

Your Sailing Environment Where are you going to go sailing? Not everyone is fortunate enough to have the Hawaiian surf and winds in their backyard. Most of us are limited to sailing at the local club, from the waterfront of our summer cottage, or at the public beach closest to home.

How often does the wind blow hard for long periods of time in your area? A visit to the local weather office will provide you with all the information you need concerning local and regional weather conditions. If the average windspeed during the summer months is less than 15 knots, it makes no sense to buy a ''high-speed'' funboard. Sailing speeds are directly dependent on wind velocity.

Price Price is the bottom line! Do you want to blow your entire budget on your first board? Or do you want to get your feet wet slowly and save some money for a second sail, or a harness and wetsuit, or maybe go south in the winter for a boardsailing vacation?

Price reflects two things: quality and sophistication of the equipment. There are low-priced boards on the market for those who want to try out the sport, and highly sophisticated, expensive boards for those who aspire to sail the waves of Hawaii.

When taken fully into consideration, these factors should help you choose the right board.

Some boardsailors prefer
large sail windows for
better visibility, particularly
when sailing downwind.

Boardsailing equipment
should be durable so that it
can be used at crowded
beaches.

Board Types

Sailboards fall under the following main categories: 1. all-round recreational boards; 2. all-round funboards or sportboards; 3. radical funboards.

All-round Recreational Boards   These boards are designed for the majority of people who take up boardsailing. Because they are very stable, they are ideal for the beginner, yet fun for the advanced sailor to sail in light winds. Their design comes from the early days of boardsailing, when most sailing was done on small inland lakes, in light winds. All-round recreational boards are equipped with a lightweight rig and a 50–60 ft² (4.5–5.5 m²) sail, ideal for learning. Optional smaller sails of 40–50 ft² (3.5–4.5 m²) are available for smaller sailors, or stronger wind, as well as a full-sized regatta sail for proficient sailors who like to race.

It is this type of board that is commonly used in one design class racing at club, national and world levels, including the 1984 Los Angeles Olympic Games.

All-round Recreational Sailboard Specifications

LENGTH:	12–12½ ft (3.7–3.9 m)
WIDTH:	26 in (66 cm)
VOLUME:	200–300 liters of flotation
WEIGHT:	44 lb (20 kg)
DESIGN CONCEPT:	Recreational sailing and racing in less than 15 knots of wind.
SAIL SIZES:	standard 50–60 ft² (4.5–5.5 m²) 1–15 knots
	regatta 65 ft² (6.0 m²) 1–15 knots
	children's 30 ft² (2.5 m²) 1–10 knots
	high wind 50 ft² (4.5 m²) up to 20 knots
SAIL DESIGN:	Horizontal or vertical cut; Dacron sailcloth.
FEATURES:	Ideal for learning, recreation and racing.

All-round Funboards or Sportboards   Funboards are slightly shorter sailboards that have a distinctive surfboard look. These boards are designed for the sailor who can handle stronger winds and is lucky enough to live where the wind blows above an average of 15 knots.

The funboard has a planing surfboard-type hull, with a pintail shape at the stern to permit surfboard-like carved turns. The deck is fitted with footstraps for control at high speeds, a retracting daggerboard and (in some models) a sliding mast track to allow adjustment of the rig for use in a wide variety of wind and water conditions. The design concept is to have a full-sized board for flotation and stability in light winds, with the adjustability to perform like a shorter board in high winds. It will not perform as well in light winds (–15 knots) as an all-round recreational board, nor as well in 15+ knots as a radical funboard.

All-round Funboard or Sportboard Specifications

LENGTH:	10–12½ ft (3.0–3.9 m)
WIDTH:	26 in (66 cm)
VOLUME:	180–250 liters of flotation
WEIGHT:	35–45 lb (15–20 kg)
DESIGN CONCEPT:	All-round use in 10–30 knots. Not for beginners.
SAIL SIZES:	65 ft² (6.0 m²) 5–15 knots
	60 ft² (5.5 m²) 15–25 knots
	55 ft² (5.0 m²) 25–30 knots
	50 ft² (4.5 m²) 30+ knots
SAIL DESIGN:	Vertical or radial cut, fathead or fully battened, using shorter booms. High aspect ratio sails. Mylar sailcloth.
FEATURES:	Fully retractable daggerboard, sliding mast track, footstraps (for strong winds). A good all-round advanced cruiser for medium winds.

Radical Funboards   The final category of sailboards are radical funboards, designed exclusively for use by accomplished board-sailors in winds in excess of 20 knots. These boards are classic surfboard shapes, capable of very high speeds and pinpoint turning, with surf sailing the main design criterion. Radical funboards come in two categories: semi-sinkers and sinkers. These ominous nautical terms refer to their flotation capabilities. Averaging 150 liters, radical funboards don't support the sailor's weight when the board is not moving. Requiring a minimum windspeed of 18 knots, this board can only be water-started and can only support the sailor when the board is moving at planing speeds — definitely not a beginner board.

Radical Funboard Specifications

LENGTH:	8–10 ft (2.4–3.0 m)
WIDTH:	22–24 in (56–61 cm)
VOLUME:	Less than 160 liters
WEIGHT:	15–25 lb (6.8–11 kg)
DESIGN CONCEPT:	High winds only, speed and radical wave maneuvers.
SAIL SIZES:	40–60 ft² (3.5–5.5 m²) 20–35 knots
SAIL DESIGN:	Vertical cut, fully battened. Mylar sailcloth.
FEATURES:	Footstraps, speed and maneuverability.
DRAWBACK:	Limited use in most inland locations, or where the wind does not average more than 15 knots.

Used Boards

In any purchase, price is always a factor and a secondhand board may be the answer for some boardsailors. A top brand sailboard loses about 10 percent of its value annually, whereas a cheaper brand can lose as much as 75 percent. To ensure that

Former world champion Rhonda Smith on one-design class equipment.

Sails should be made from a durable material such as Dacron or Mylar, and all high stress areas (tack, clew, batten pockets and top of the mast sleeve) should be reinforced.

you are getting top quality for your dollar, the purchase of a used board should be done through a dealer. Generally, look for a molded plastic hull, aluminum booms and, if you are small in stature, a small rather than a full-sized sail.

Hull   Look the hull over for cracks and tears. Tears allow water to be absorbed by the foam core. A good indication of water retention is the weight of the board. Lift the board up and see if it weighs more than you think it should. Run your hands over the upper- and undersurfaces of the hull to check for soft or spongy areas. Compare it to other boards in the store or check the specifications for new boards.

Daggerboard and Skeg   The daggerboard is a good indication of the care given the board by the previous owner. If it is damaged, you can assume that the board has been run aground.

Look for tears in the daggerboard well. If there are cracks, you can be sure water has seeped into the foam core. Again, if possible, weigh the board.

Take a skeg key or screwdriver along with you when purchasing a used board. Unscrew the skeg and check that there are no cracks or holes in the fin box.

Mast Assembly   Watch for tape around the bottom of the mast and remove it to check for splits in the fiberglass material. Damage is most common in the bottom of the mast and the part of the mast where the boom is attached. Look these areas over carefully for any signs of wear and tear. Check the universal joint for sand and see that it rotates freely.

Booms   Immerse aluminum booms, if possible, to see if they are taking in water. Cracked, split or damaged material in the booms is a good indication that the boom may be absorbing water. Check the inhaul and outhaul cleats to make sure they are secure and not worn out.

Maintenance of Equipment

Boardsailing equipment is easy to maintain. After sailing on the ocean, or a lake for that matter, you should remove all sand from all moving parts, the hull and the sail. This will increase the length of time your equipment will last.

Any cracks that appear in the hull should be repaired immediately to prevent water from being absorbed by the foam core. You can fix cracks yourself using a hot-melt (thermoplastic) glue gun and all-purpose glue sticks. If you aren't adept at repair work, it's best to approach a dealer about repairs.

Ocean sailors should remove salt from their equipment to prevent corrosion.

Keep your sail out of the sun for long periods, because ultraviolet light will make the sail brittle. Dry the sail before placing it in a sail bag and be sure to take the battens out before folding and storing your sail. When your sailboard is rigged but not in use, slacken the downhaul and outhaul lines.

Storage of the board is simple. Place it on its edge on a flat, dry surface.

CHAPTER 12

What to Wear

Safety is the major factor to consider when purchasing this part of your boardsailing equipment. Since the sailboard is an extremely wet boat, care must be taken to guarantee adequate warmth and buoyancy capabilities in your clothing.

Mike Gadd and Carol Taylor wear full wetsuits.

Swimsuits

Swimsuits are suitable for boardsailing only when the air temperature is above 80°F (27°C), and the water is above 75°F (24°C). If you spend a lot of time in the water as opposed to sailing, the wind will evaporate the water from your skin, causing a dramatic drop in body temperature. Top sailors in Hawaii often wear a neoprene vest or shortie wetsuit when the wind is in excess of 20 knots.

Wetsuits

An essential accessory for extending the boardsailing season beyond the warm summer months, and a way to make those windy, cold summer days more pleasurable, is the wetsuit. The combination of wind and water can cause a loss of body heat, which in turn can cause a loss of energy. This may lead to intense chilling and possibly hypothermia (see Appendix 1). A wetsuit will help prevent this problem.

A combination john and jacket wetsuit.

The wetsuit provides a layer of insulation between the body and the suit. This minimizes heat loss from the body. Neoprene, a synthetic rubber filled with tiny air or nitrogen bubbles, is the most commonly used material for wetsuits. It is very elastic and although it is not an approved PFD (personal flotation device) it provides a certain amount of buoyancy.

Pure neoprene provides the best type of insulation, but it is not durable enough to use alone in a suit. A synthetic lining, such as nylon or lycra, is essential on the inside for added strength. Suits that are lined on both sides are more durable, but do not insulate as well as suits that are lined on one side. The reason for this is that an external synthetic lining absorbs water while the shiny black neoprene lets it run off. Heat loss through evaporation is therefore much higher for the double-lined suits. Suits with a rough-textured neoprene on the outside are not as warm as those with a smooth neoprene because the water does not run off as easily.

Both types of wetsuits are usually warm enough in cool weather conditions. If you do not plan to sail in cold temperatures, the choice between the two types is an aesthetic one. Suits that are lined on two sides can be many different colors, whereas neoprene on one side has only one color — black. Combinations with double lining on specific parts of the suit are also available.

The thickness of the neoprene suit depends on the severity of the conditions. Neoprene wetsuits were originally designed for divers. The boardsailing suit doesn't have to be as thick as a diving suit because the boardsailor spends more time out of the water than in the water. A 3/16 in (.32 cm) thickness is recommended because it does not inhibit the mobility required in boardsailing.

The wetsuit allows a thin layer of water between the neoprene and the body. The thinner the layer of water, the better. A tight fit is

A drysuit.

A short-sleeved wetsuit.

therefore mandatory. The fit should be snug around the groin and shoulder areas, but looser under the arms and in the knee area. Be sure to check for abrasive seams.

For most northern sailing conditions, a combination john and jacket suit is ideal. When john and jacket are worn together, the insulation factor is warm enough for air temperatures down to 70°F (21°C). These suits are available in colors or in a plain black neoprene. In windy summer or tropical conditions, a vest or shortie suit will take care of any wind chill through evaporation.

Drysuits

As the name implies, drysuits keep you dry. Watertight, and designed to be worn over thermal underwear or other clothing, a drysuit can keep you comfortable in temperatures down to 50°F (10°C). Avid sailors wear drysuits to extend the sailing season in spring and fall.

Other Equipment

Other equipment is available to the boardsailor to make the sport more pleasurable. For example, if you find your feet get cold on cool days, you could invest in a pair of neoprene boots. Running shoes will do if you don't want to buy boots; however, they obviously won't be as warm.

On long sails, gloves can prevent calluses and blisters. Specially designed gloves for boardsailing are on the market; however, some boardsailors use sailing gloves or gloves that gymnasts use. These can be purchased at most sporting goods stores.

To avoid sunstroke, it's always a good idea to wear a visor. Visors are available from most dealers.

In some areas you are required by law to wear a PFD (personal flotation device). The kind you buy should be comfortable and government approved. A tested, government-approved jacket will keep the head above water, increasing survival time in cold water.

Running shoes can be worn to keep the feet warm.

To avoid sunstroke, it's a
good idea to wear a visor.

Appendices

Hypothermia

Hypothermia is much more than feeling a chill. It's a killer. If a boardsailor doesn't know how to cope with this particular condition, death is not unlikely.

Hypothermia occurs when intense cold attacks the major core areas of the body, such as the heart and brain. Clinically, heat is lost within the body at a faster rate than it can be regenerated by burning food and fat reserves.

An individual in the state of hypothermia will undergo a number of physical and mental changes. In extremely cold water the body reacts to protect itself. Shivering is one sign of hypothermia. The body shivers as a means of creating heat to stop the fall of the core body temperature. Blood supply to the extremities is reduced and body metabolism is increased through a higher breathing rate and heartbeat. These reactions occur because the body is trying to protect the heart and brain from heat loss.

Hands and feet lose heat at a high rate because of their cylindrical shape. The high heat loss in these areas causes a reduction in manual dexterity, touch discrimination and movement in the muscles and joints.

Cold water quickly drains an individual's strength, and swimming 100 yd (91 m) or climbing out of the water becomes almost impossible. Mentally, there is an overriding sensation of pain. According to Joseph McInnis in *The icy facts on how cold water kills*, "Anxiety and confusion are mixed with a feeling of impending doom, particularly if help is not at arm's length away. Judgment, memory and reason are impaired and within minutes the individual is teetering on the abyss of panic."

The survival time in cold water depends upon the weight of the individual (heavier people have more fat that can be regenerated into heat), the temperature of the water and the person's physical capabilities.

Survival time is increased if the sailor gets out of the water by climbing on top of the hull. Heat loss in the air is less than heat loss in the water.

There are two main areas of the body that suffer high heat loss: the sides of the chest and the groin region. To prevent heat loss in these areas, hold the inner sides of the arms tightly against the chest and press the thighs together and raise them to close off the groin area.

If you see someone suffering from hypothermia, check for a doctor in the area and call an ambulance to move the person to a hospital.

To rewarm a victim of hypothermia, huddle people together around the victim. Place hot, wet towels, water bottles, electric and chemical heating pads or heated blankets on the individual. Hot, non-alcoholic drinks and a hot bath or shower may also help.

Be sure that you don't rub the surface of the victim's body or jolt him or her in any way.

Before you go out boardsailing, check the weather and water temperature carefully. During cold water and weather conditions wear a neoprene wetsuit or a drysuit to prevent rapid heat loss. Also make sure that there is a retrieval boat close at hand so that if you do get into trouble on the water there is someone to pick you up. Most of all, use common sense.

Boardsailing on Ice and Snow

Iceboating is the sailor's winter alternative. This option is also open to the boardsailor who can hook his or her sail to a variety of craft and sail at 40 m.p.h. (64 k.p.h.) over the ice. Snowboards made of polyethylene (the same material used in ski bases) will move much more quickly than on water, approaching 30 knots of speed.

A word of caution. There obviously is risk involved in careening across a hard medium while standing up and trying to hang onto a runaway sail. Helmets and elbow pads are recommended to provide adequate body protection.

As the board begins to move in even the lightest of winds, the friction between the runners and the ice is so minimal that the board accelerates instantly to five times windspeed. Apparent wind plays a very important role in sail control when such speeds are attained.

There are a number of sailboard icecraft commercially available. Most are made to accommodate sailboard rigs. Some rigs can be screwed on. However, the design is quite elementary, and a comparable apparatus can be built for very little money. Simply cut a 5 ft 9 in (1.75 m) long, 3 ft (1 m) wide triangle of thick plywood and add angle iron runners at each corner, sharpening the rear two for a good grip on the ice to keep the craft from slipping sideways. The dull-edged front runner allows the bow of the board to be pushed laterally by the legs. The sharp rear runners assume the function and position of a daggerboard on a water hull. A pair of well-sharpened skis fixed slightly on edge to the platform work well on snow.

As mentioned above, polyethylene snowboards will slide over the snow, but not as quickly as hulls equipped with runners will slide over ice. A fun day of fast reaching will prompt most aficionados to devise an icecraft suited to speed and performance.

Boardsailing on ice should be done in a large open area of clear ice, free of snow patches and any obstacles, moving or stationary. These craft are not as maneuverable as aquatic hulls and require much more room to tack, jibe and come to a stop, in part because of the higher speeds involved. Don't go off chasing snowmobiles and iceboats until you've had an opportunity to practice the basic skills!

Northern sailors whose lakes freeze, but don't receive much snow cover, are in an ideal situation to expand their fleet activities into the winter months. Patchy or solid snow-covered ice will inhibit performance, but with a hybrid snow-ice boat on very shallow runners, good performance can be expected in less than ideal conditions.

Ice sailing is only recommended for advanced sailors. High wind experience is necessary to handle the higher windspeeds involved. Intermediate boardsailors should only try ice sailing with very small sails to keep the speed down.

Glossary

Aft   Toward the stern of the sailboard.
Apparent wind   A change in wind direction caused by the forward speed of the board.
Astern - Behind the stern.
Backwinding   Occurs when the board is going faster than the true wind, causing the opposite side of the sail to fill with air.
Beam reach   A course 90° from the wind.
Bear off   To change course away from the wind.
Beat   Sail upwind. Also the upwind leg of a race.
Bow   The forwardmost part of the hull.
Broad reach   A course aft of 90° from the wind.
Clear (or clean) air   Wind that is not affected by other boards or obstructions.
Cleat   A small plastic device to which a line is tied. Securing a line on a cleat.
Clew   The lower corner of the sail which is farthest from the mast.
Close hauled   Sailing as close to the wind as possible.
Close reach   A course forward of 90° from the wind.
Dirty air   Wind that has been affected by other boards or obstructions.
Downwind   Away from the direction from which the wind is blowing.
Fore   Toward the bow of the board.
Head off   See **bear off**.
Head to wind   On a course that is heading directly into the wind.
Head up   To change course toward the wind.
Heading   A point on the horizon to sail toward.
Hull drag   Frictional resistance on the hull caused by the movement of the hull through the water.
Jibe   To bring the board around onto a new course by turning the hull downwind and around onto the new course.
Knot   One nautical mile (6060 ft/1847 m) per hour.

Lateral resistance   The hull slides to leeward while sailing. This is counteracted by the size and shape of the daggerboard.
Leech   The edge of the sail between the head and the clew.
Leeward   Away from the wind. The downwind side of anything.
Luff   A sail will luff or flap loosely when it is not completely full of wind.
Mark   A marker or buoy that sailboards sail around in a race.
Offshore wind   Blowing away from the shoreline.
Onshore wind   Blowing from the water to the land.
Pinch   To sail too close to the wind, preventing the board from making progress upwind.
Point   To sail close hauled.
Port   The left side of a board when viewed from the stern.
Port tack   When the wind is filling the left side of the sail and the left hand is closest to the mast, the board is said to be on a port tack.
Railing up   The hull flips up onto its side or rail.
Rake   To lean the sail to port, starboard, fore or aft.
Reach   A course across the wind. See **beam reach, broad reach** and **close reach**.
Running with (or before) the wind   Sailing with the wind blowing directly behind the board.
Sheet in   To fill the sail with more air by pulling the sail in with the aft hand.
Sheet out   To dump wind from the sail by easing the sail out with the aft hand.
Spill wind   See **sheet out**.
Starboard   The right side of a board when viewed from the stern.
Starboard tack   When the wind is filling the right side of the sail and the right hand is closest to the mast, the board is said to be on a starboard tack.

Stern   The aftermost part of the hull.

Tack   The lower corner of the sail which is closest to the mast. Being on a tack is sailing a constant course. Tacking in boardsailing is bringing the board around onto a new course by turning the hull up into the wind, stepping around the front of the mast to the opposite side of the sail and bearing off onto the new course.

Trimming the sail   Sheeting in or out to obtain maximum power from the wind. Fine-tuning the sail.

True wind   The wind that is felt on a board that is not moving. See **apparent wind**.

Upwind   Toward the direction from which the wind is blowing.

Weather, to   See **upwind**.

Wind shift   A change in the direction of the wind.

Windward   Toward the wind. The upwind side of anything.

Index

Photo Credits